ENTERTAINMENT DINING

MARTIN M. PEGLER

ENTERTAINMENT DINING

MARTIN M. PEGLER

VISUAL REFERENCE PUBLICATIONS, INC.

NEW YORK

Visual Reference Publications

302 Fifth Avenue

New York, NY 10001

Distributors to the trade in the United States and Canada

Watson-Guptill Publishers

1515 Broadway

New York, NY 10036

Distributors outside the United Sates and Canada

Hearst Books International

1350 Avenue of the Americas

New York, NY 10019

Library of Congress Cataloging in Publication Data:

Entertainment Dining

Printed in Hong Kong

ISBN 1–58471–005–5

Designed by Dutton & Sherman

TABLE OF CONTENTS

INTRODCUTION

John Rancanelli of Rancanelli Development, a company that consists of several upscale restaurants, said, "Design attracts people to a restaurant the first time and sometimes the second but the food has to follow up strongly to keep them coming back." In all probabilities, it is our sense of taste that decides whether or not we return to a restaurant again and again, but with our lives so controlled and oriented by entertainment and the stimulation of all our other senses, the ambiance is very important.

What makes for an "entertaining dining experience"? It can be a theme restaurant filled with Hollywood memorabilia, flashing lights and TV monitors playing endless replays of familiar scenes from familiar movies or it can be a visit to a foreign or exotic place without packing a suitcase or even showing a passport. We can be transported to a mountain village in Tuscany or sit on a veranda in the Serengeti watching digitized animals moving all around us. Ever wanted to descend to the depths without getting wet or using snorkeling equipment? How about visiting Machu Picchu and never being troubled by the altitude? Well, you can do all that in one visit to the Cafe Odyssey in the Mall of America. Would you like your sushi or shashumi served authentically but not have to pay for the airfare to Japan? There are places you can try on Sullivan St. in New York City or in West Los Angeles. Foreign and exotic atmospheric elements can make ethnic foods seem so much more "authentic" and enjoyable. It is entertainment!

ACTION—we seek the lights and some of us don't even mind if the camera is on us and we are "the show." But, how many more of us prefer to be the audience and watch the varied and always new show being cooked up and performed in the open / exhibition kitchens? Whether it is chefs preparing dishes with flair and flourish, pizzas being tossed and turned and then baked in wood burning ovens, or salads whipped up flavored with a dash of panache—it's always fun and awesome to watch the professionals doing their thing. If you want to play "a supporting role," some of the new restaurants put you into the act. You select the ingredients for your "dish" and then bring it to the wok or grill chef where he/she finishes it off before your very eyes—and the eyes of all the other diners. This is about as close as you can get to being on stage and yet stay out of the spotlights. That's entertainment!

People watching people watching people can also be a source of dining entertainment. It's the reason people withstand the fumes of passing cars and the attacks of occasional pigeons to dine in crushing sidewalk cafes. What better place for people watching—in all weather—than in brewpubs and wine bars? If you want to be less obvious you can always seem to be studying the brewing and bottling processes going on just beyond the wide expanses of glass that separate the dining/drinking patron from the real, live action-filled micro brewing that is a real attraction to many . That's entertainment!

In this edition of Entertainment Dining, we have tried to include many of these entertainment factors that tend to enhance the dining experience.

We hope you enjoy this gastronomic tour of our garden of culinary delights and that you will gather from these projects and pictures some of the smells, sights, and feelings of fun and excitement that have made these restaurants, cafes, grills and pubs so successful . These are places where patrons return again and again for the food—and the changing entertainment.

Martin M. Pegler

ENTERTAINMENT DINING

MARTIN M. PEGLER

CAFE ODYSSEY

BLOOMINGTON, MN

Design:
Cuningham Group, Minneapolis, MN

Lead Designer:
Patrick Huss

Show Manager:
Steven Lynch

Lead Interior Designer:
Jan Dufault

Design/Building Project Manager:
Jeffrey Stebbins

Project Team:
Pat Mackey/Dan Drescher/Todd Hesson/Nancy Ohm/Dave Stephani/Dave Kulich/John Rezab/Pat Martin/Dawn Wieczorek/Ted Steiner

Photography:
Dana Wheelock, Wheelock Photography

The client wanted an interactive, multi-themed restaurant that would reflect a whimsical sense of mystery and adventure. What they got is the 16,215 sq. ft. Cafe Odyssey— located in the Mall of America in Bloomington, MN. Here guests are invited to explore, experience and enjoy the view from a veranda overlooking the plains of the Serengeti or sit amid the ruins of the ancient Incan city of Machu Picchu in Peru. They can also opt to find themselves in the mythical city of Atlantis. Each dining room

combines theater, multi-media and design elements for an experience that is truly different.

Dark wood paneling and rich colored slate floors with custom carpets set the scene at the entrance. The Explorer's Bar is filled with mahogany wood, trophy heads of animals and an oversized globe. It is the essence of the "men's club" of another period with swirling blue, green and gold slate floors that suggest "flow and movement" while the reddish cherry wood tones add a feeling of warmth.

"Atlantis is a sanctuary" where diners sit in booths ensconced in coral beds while digitally composed "fish" swim by in the undersea setting. The deep blue carpeting has a wave-like pattern and seemingly crumbling columns interrupt and define the space. The lighting fixtures resemble coral and jelly fish-like creatures.

The patterns and colors of Machu Picchu celebrate the natives and the greenery of the Andes mountains and here the diners look out over the ruins of an ancient city. Water flows from an unseen source into pools located near the tables.

The plains of the Serengeti can be seen through the ornate iron gates that surround the veranda where patrons

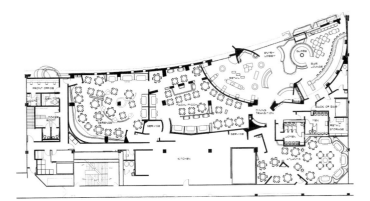

are seated. Digitally composed wildlife travel across the large projection screen. A tall, reedy trunked acacia tree is centered in this area and it is in full foliage. Here, too, patterns and materials are based on those native to the African locale.

As in all Cuningham Group themed entertainment projects, Cafe Odyssey began with the scripting of a highly developed "back story": a narrative approach to design that engages guests on more than the superficial level of themed restaurants. A major feature in each area is a "living mural": a video projection into artwork that depicts backgrounds, changing times of day, and small "events" appropriate to each locale.

MARS 2112

NEW YORK, NY

Entertainment Design and Architecture:
Daroff Design, Inc.
DDI Architects P.C.
Philadelphia PA.

Principals in charge:
Karen Daroff
James Rappoport, AIA

Design Director:
Martin Komitzky

Project Manager/Architect:
Edgar Dale, AIA

Senior Designer:
Richard Marencic

Design Team:
Barry Corson/Katherine Bottom/Dave Layton/
Roger Acuna/Christine Neilon/Joe Fattore/Karen
Pelzer/Glen Swantak/Simone Makoul

Client:
Paschal Phelan, Albert Lennon

Photographer:
Peter Paige Interior Photography,
Harrington Park, NJ

Located in the center of New York's Entertainment district is an entertainment/eatery venue that is literally a trip to outer space. This hyper intensive, all enveloping and all entertaining 32,000 sq. ft. facility starts with a "spaceship" which hovers in the Plaza pit. Guests are led towards this vehicle and into an Earth Spaceport where they receive their tickets for the journey to Mars. Two "space shuttles" provide the transport for 25 guests each, and after a four minute "ride"—they arrive in Mars.

The arrival zone is reminiscent of the settings for "Blade Runner" and "Men in Black." The passageway resembles a fiery cave and the "space travellers" are required to walk across pontoons floating in "lava" or some other "liquid space substance" to arrive at the overlook of a crater. Guests can be seated in the 114-seat mezzanine Crater Dining Room or descend to the crater's 300-seat base via a grand staircase.

Crater Dining Room guests are surrounded by red rock formations, "Mercury Xenon" crystal trees and other Martian "sights." Through the "Window to Mars," diners can enjoy ever changing views of the Martian landscape. A Martian MC or VJ guides guests through a meteor shower "where the artificial environment of the crater is threatened and the air and water 'systems' are damaged." Fortunately, Martian drones toil tirelessly and endlessly to "save the earthlings" so that they can come back again to visit Mars 2112.

After the thorough dining/entertainment experience, patrons are transported back to "Earth" with a detour to a well stocked and amusingly themed retail store for the all important "mementos" of the journey.

Mars 2112 has truly sent shock-waves down Broadway and has garnered design awards along the way for Daroff Design of Philadelphia, including the Best Themed Venue of the Year from *Nightclub & Bar Magazine*.

FANTASEA REEF

ATLANTIC CITY, NJ

Entertainment Design and Architecture:
Daroff Design, Inc.
DDI Architects P.C.
Philadelphia PA.

Principals in Charge:
Karen Daroff
James Rappoport, AIA

Design Director:
Martin Komitzky

Project Manager:
Gregg Olmstead

Project Architect:
Scott Winger

Senior Designers:
Martin Komitzky
Richard Marencic

Graphic Design/Signage:
Simone Makoul

Interior Architecture:
Arthur W. Ponzio & Co., Atlantic City, NJ

Photography:
Elliott Kaufman, New York, NY

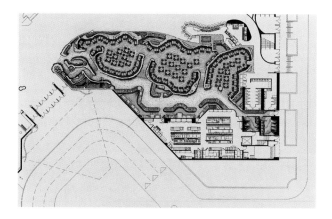

Daroff Design of Philadelphia was commissioned by Harrah's to integrate the marine theme throughout their Atlantic City hotel/casino, and it culminates in the award winning Fantasea Reef restaurant. The 14,000 sq. ft. space, themed as a coral reef, is located adjacent to the expanded casino entrance.

Upon entering the 400-seat buffet restaurant, diners first encounter Marina and King Neptune, who guide them through a simulated underwater tunnel which is surrounded by a giant tropical fish aquarium. The diners exit into za dramatically illuminated 24 ft. high space where huge, free-formed, arched theatrical coral reefs envelop them. These elements were built and molded on-site: structural mesh armatures were sheathed in concrete, then textured and painted to simulate an actual under-water reef.

"We wanted to create a completely hyper-immersive experience. As in nature, everything is organic and irregular with no rectilinear edges. The emphasis is on comfort and a positive guest experience," says Karen Daroff.

Ten ft. high faux sea kelp, hundreds of hand blown, colorful translucent glass fish suspended from the ceiling along with sculptural coral pieces, and glistening fiber optic sea anemones all add to the underwater ambience. In addition, there are three dimensional "murals," video walls, glowing bubble coral and more aquariums. To enhance the underwater fantasy adventure and the overall guest experience, blue cathode lighting and other special lighting effects suggest the colors and the movements of the ocean.

Daroff Design also created the hand painted, resin finished table tops that further reflect the coral formations. Whimsical, curved wood dining chairs remind one of an

octopus or sea creature, and the custom pattern carpet design suggests the ocean floor by using sea kelp green, sand and coral tones.

Daroff Design also coordinated the work of a team of creative specialists, consultants, artisans, skilled sub-contractors and suppliers. "While we were creating this sense of illusion," Daroff says, "we were supported by Harrah's in-house entertainment division, which used the latest audio-visual technology, including sound effects from the ocean. It's a multi-media, multi-sensory experience."

The adventure is underscored with soft, non-obtrusive sounds. "We aren't attempting to recreate a locale that already exists, but evoke the feelings people get when they visit an exciting place," Daroff says.

Fantasea Reef is consistently rated the best buffet restaurant in Atlantic City, and its design is clearly a key to its success. According to *Casino Player's* "Best of Gaming '99" issue, Harrah's "wondrous 'under the sea' spectacle" is "nothing short of stunning, and clearly part of the reason why the Fantasea Reef is so popular."

THE RESTAURANTS AT CAESAR'S PALACE

ATLANTIC CITY, NJ

Design:
Brennan Beer Gorman Monk, New York, NY

Photography:
Tom Crane

Located on the casino level of the recently expanded and renovated Caesar's Palace in Atlantic City is the 144-seat Rotunda Restaurant and the Bacchus Bar that can accommodate 120. The largest dining area, Café Roma with a seating capacity of 250 is located on the third floor of the new Centurion Tower. Neo-classically inspired, they carry through the majesty and opulence of the theme—Caesar's classic Rome—as interpreted by BBGM of New York.

The Temple Lobby sets the look for the new Caesar's and is also the focal point: a four story, 29,000 sq. ft. "celebration of Roman architectural antiquity." It is a grandiose space and filled with elements that take the visitor back in time to the glorious period: statues, columns, fountains, building facades, balconies and cornices that all echo the grandeur of ancient Rome.

The Rotunda Restaurant has a nine ft. diameter astroglobe, forged in metal, centered beneath a 16 ft. dome which is supported by fluted Corinthian columns. The ceiling is a velvety evening sky accented with an astrological motif which is also repeated on the carpeting and the upholstery fabrics.

The two-level Bacchus Bar is distinguished by a black and gold palette. The colors appear in a variety of patterns such as stripes and diamonds used on the upholstery, and the tiger-striped carpeting. The fluted columns are enriched with gold ornamentation as are the ebonized wood seats. In the niches, above the banquette seating, there are classically inspired custom created murals.

The casual and large Café Roma is redolent in red and gold with a printed red carpet and the ceiling painted a Pompeian red color. The walls are faux finished in a mottled ocher gold which is accented by the dark mahogany millwork. The same dark color is used for the serving bars, the tables and the chairs.

MARVEL MANIA

UNIVERSAL CITY, CA

Design:
The Rockwell Group, New York, NY
David Rockwell

Photography:
Paul Warchol, New York, NY

The design challenge presented to the noted theme restaurant design firm, The Rockwell Group of New York, was to translate the Marvel comic book universe into a three dimensional form, "while preserving the element of imagination which is central to the spirited and fanciful art of the printed comic book page."

To accomplish this feat, the designers utilized a play between three dimensional realizations against two dimensional artwork. Large scale, high quality painted murals create exciting and space altering effects and overscaled cut-out images of superheroes and villains "float within hybrid environments of dimensional form with drawn detailing." The overall effect, according to the designers, is of "a fluid, changing reality."

Located on the entertainment oriented City Walk in Universal City, CA, the restaurant has a fabulous, colorful and exciting facade as well as two entrances. Guests are

invited to pass through the "Decompression Chamber," a first experience, and either have a drink at the Villain's Bar or play a "Trivia" game which is projected on the dome of the Iron Mask Hall. There is also a display of weaponry and costume technology in "fantasy Cryogenic cases" which also contain Capt. Marvel artifacts.

The dining room offers the diner a choice of realms: Danger Dining Room, Comic Book Dining, the Control Room, or the Black Bird Cock Pit. In the Control Room there is a show that features story lines that seem to emanate from the screen and that cause lighting and sound effects that are heard and seen throughout the dining space. The Morph Wall surrounds the screen and it is a translucent, faceted surface which is capable of receiving back and front projection in concert with the story line.

As a fun touch, there are changing, "thought balloons" that hover over the diners' heads and they pretend to illustrate what the different patrons are thinking. The diners are surrounded by the entertainment values of the Marvel Comics.

In the retail store, three dimensional reproductions of the superheros are set against a graphic floor treatment. The fun continues into the restrooms which are themed as "biohazard zones," and here are featured custom Marvel video shorts with superheros making appearances from behind semi-mirrored doors. But—it is all entertainment!

BET SOUNDSTAGE

LARGO, MD

Design:
Lawson Design Corp., Annapolis, MD
George Lawson/Kendyl Lawson/Jeffrey
Steir/Wendy Weller

Photography:
Stewart Brothers Photography, Inc.

The soundstage concept, as envisioned by the architectural design firm Lawson Design Corp. of Annapolis, MD, was the ideal solution for Black Entertainment Television's theme restaurant. Not only did it relate directly to the cable TV company, it also allowed for a variety of "sets" within the space. The original concept was then expanded to incorporate interactive TV.

The prototype theme restaurant was built in Largo, MD, a suburb of Washington, DC, and the exterior of the building with its illuminated marquee and neon signage recalls the excitement and grandeur of an earlier Hollywood. There is a walk-of-fame with plaques honoring black artists such as Michael Jordan and Whitney Houston. The lobby makes a striking statement in chrome, glass, steel and dramatic lighting. Moats, surrounding the sloping floor, make the ramp appear suspended while the pol-

ished black granite flooring creates a modern/high tech
entranceway. The maitre d' stand is located at the end of
the ramp and it is backed up by a two story director's
booth. The BET Soundstage logo is prominently displayed
throughout: sandblasted into the lobby floor, engraved on
brass plaques, etched in glass panels and in the signage.
Just off the lobby is the entrance to the retail store where
more of the logo appears on the fun casual wear and souvenirs.

The 24 ft. high ceiling in the restaurant creates a sense
of vastness, yet the designers were able to inject a feeling
of intimacy in the peripheral seating where raised plat-
forms and lowered ceilings combine to form individual
stage set environments. The sets include an art deco
vignette, the pergolla, and an urban metropolitan scene
with steel beams and articulated columns. The settings are
defined by a metropolis '40s World's Fair architectural
facade, an art deco marquee and a radio tower with blink-
ing aircraft warning lights.

The central area houses the bar and above it are the
catwalks to service the theatrical lights and cameras that

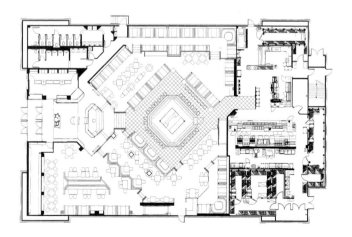

give real meaning to the concept and the guests' experiences. The designers selected custom dyed carpeting for the "blue screen" wall and floors. The sound stage imagery is further enhanced by the six light towers and the robotic cameras on tracks. The audio/visual system and the cameras are controlled from the director's booth that was first seen in the lobby. Three large video walls are strategically placed to have a strong presence and yet blend with the restaurant setting. Throughout the design rich and beautiful materials are employed such as solid mahogany railings and table tops, and marble and granite floors. African slate is used on a lower video wall to create texture and color.

The lighting plays a vital part in projecting the theme and mostly theatrical lighting fixtures were used as they are in TV productions. "The light creates excitement and a sense of theater." At BET Soundstage the guests provide the entertainment. It is "Candid Camera" time and you can be the one the camera is on! But, there is always a new "script"—a new "cast" and the "show" is always new.

PROPS

CHARLOTTE, NC

Design:
Shook Design Group, Charlotte, NC

Photography:
Tim Buchman Photography

The objective was to create an eating environment that would seat up to 300 guests in an underperforming restaurant space located in a virtually hidden site—and do it on a limited budget. Shook Design Group of Charlotte, NC took up the challenge with the proviso that they would have the privilege of creating the entire concept: the name, layout, format, and even the menu.

The design concept for Props is based on the popular TV series "Friends" and the restaurant is targeted at the

audience that faithfully follows the lives of the TV "friends."
They are smart young professionals in their 20s and early
30s. According to the designers, "More than any other gen-
eration in the last 30 years, this group represents a major
cultural paradigm shift in eating habits and preferences:
they rarely eat at home; they eat differently than their parents; they are seeking 'real' places; and they crave socially
conducive environments."

The design solution is based on creating a series of
"living room" vignettes composed entirely of flea market
furniture that "urges social interaction." Like the ambiance,
the food is eclectic and encourages group participation.
The unique and ever changing landscape of the dining
space which is theatrically and inexpensively divided into
smaller and more intimate dining spaces has proven to be
a source of entertainment for diners. Here they discover
the pleasures of the actual dining experience.

PROPS RESTAURANT

The restaurant almost resembles a TV or movie studio where diners are invited to move from one stage set to the next. The settings are differentiated by floor-to-ceiling fabric panels of strong colors, theatrical flats, swags and drapes, makeshift skeletal constructions, mache or fiberglass overscaled props, changes in flooring materials, or levels on the floor. The lighting is low, intimate and theatrical like the space. The exposed warehouse ceiling, the ducts and pipes and wiring overhead are all painted black to disappear into a void.

Dining at Props is not only cozy, comfortable and an experience but also a moment "on stage" where you have entered the world behind the TV screen, the diner becomes a performer and maybe even "a star."

ELVIS PRESLEY'S MEMPHIS

MEMPHIS, TN

Design:
Aumiller Youngquist, Mt. Prospect, IL

Design:
Idea, Inc., Orlando, FL

Architect:
Hnedak Bobo Group, Memphis, TN

Photographer:
Todd Winters

What would be a more natural coupling than a 330-seat restaurant/entertainment venue for live musical performances on historic Beale St. and the Elvis Presley name?

The first step into the three story building, which was originally a clothing store where Presley bought the suit he wore on the Ed Sullivan show, is a reflection of Elvis' flashy taste: the theatrical glitzy style he made his signature. Inlaid in the floor is a lightning bolt which was Elvis' "takin' care of business" sign. The T.C.B. logo is also featured in one of the rooms on the second level. The focal centerpiece of the interior is the two level space with the open stage. Since the stage is so important for the entertainment, "The Memphis Show Room," as designed by Aumiller Youngquist, features high backed, round booths and high gloss black tables to show the Las Vegas influ-

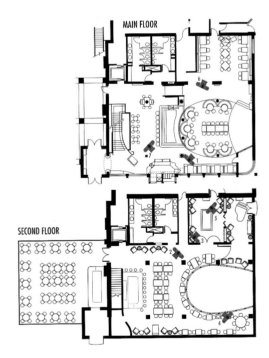

MAIN FLOOR

SECOND FLOOR

ence in this memorial/theme/restaurant dedicated to Presley. According to Keith Aumiller, the booths not only help to define the space but also make it appear more comfortable as a dining area. The fabulous, ornate crystal and gilt chandelier that hangs over the high open space with its black and white checkered floor is one of 32 originally designed for a Saudi prince.

Beyond the brick pillars that are original to the building is the "706 Music Library." Here, old haberdashery cabinets hold the extensive collection of Presley records and books. The Sun Studio at 706 Union St. is where Elvis cut his first record and thus the name of the room. On the second level in the T.C.B. Lounge, in addition to such precious memorabilia as Elvis' jumpsuit, leather jacket and guitar, there is the "King's" own pool table which he and the Beatles played on. The fabric covered walls here, as well as in other areas of the restaurant, were inspired by those in the billiard room in Graceland. The domed ceiling is painted like a night sky. Some of the furnishings here, come from Elvis' and his parents' homes. The restaurant's V.I.P. lounge, "The Eagle's Nest" is filled with photographs of Elvis and his multitude of important celebrity friends. Here, too, the furniture is authentic Presley owned.

The success of the restaurant and the attached retail store for souvenir items has convinced the management to build three more Elvis Presley's Memphis units in the next two years.

HARLEY DAVIDSON CAFE

LAS VEGAS, NV

Design:
Haverson Architecture & Design, Greenwich, CT

Photography:
Pall Warchol, New York, NY

Making a statement amid the many other illuminated and flickering "statements" on the Las Vegas strip is the new Harley Davidson Cafe designed by Haverson Architecture & Design. The larger-than-life, authentically replicated motorcycle takes center stage as an American trophy on a canopy above the entry to the cafe. "The bike appears as though emerging, unbridled and free, from the truncated corner of the building." The balance of the facade is that of a proud "vintage American" building: a fitting background to a great American product.

Pedestrian traffic, on the strip, is redirected by the landscaping with bikes seemingly overgrown with topiary and also by the 100 ft. animated strip sign. Guests entering "ride" in on Rte 66—a map that colorfully animates the ceiling and highlights famous, well traveled road sites where races and bike rallies are traditionally held. Immediately to the right of the entrance is the retail shop which is stocked

with Harley Davidson Cafe caps, tee shirts, and other mementos. Non-diners can also access the store directly from the street. The Harley Davidson credo—"Live Free, Ride Free"—is inlaid in the semi-circular entry flooring. Also evident in the entry is the flag: "the flag is alive with American spirit, as a sequential display of lighting effects animate the colors of the oversized, undulating flag." Once inside, the guest can see the Rte. 66 Bar, the main dining room and "an authentic demonstration of a motorcycle assembly line featuring the most current HD models journeying overhead throughout the restaurant." They are attached to a track above by means of steel harnesses. The fleet of bikes becomes a source of entertainment as they steadily move through various areas of the restaurant, at both levels, and at times disappear behind walls or through the floor" to create a fun and varied visual experience."

The bar stools of the Rte 66 Bar imitate motorcycle seats, and windshields lined up like bikes in a row help to separate the bar area from the dining room. The palette of materials used to finish the interior space includes stainless steel and chrome used on hand railings and stair construction, and warm, medium colored woods on a high wainscot

against which images of HD celebrity owners from the world of sports, Hollywood, and Rock 'n Roll appear. The floor coverings vary from cracked tiles and wood finishes to "road patterned" carpeting. A vintage pantinaed wallcovering—like aged plaster—is used on the walls and ceiling while dark, leather-like material, channeled or tufted with studs cover the banquettes and column enclosures. The colors and materials "reflect the same manufacturing know-how and high quality craftsmanship used in building the HD motorcycle."

Low voltage lighting, designed in the shape of Harley headlights, tail lights and engine blocks, are used as sconces and hanging sprocket pendants. HD gas tanks, signed by celebrities line the walls along with logo images. Other sources of entertainment in the cafe include video events shown on conveniently placed monitors, custom bikes, a diorama built around Ann Margaret and her Harley bike in a Las Vegas state setting, and a collage of HD seen through photos, poster art and 3D artifacts.

"Visitors to the Harley Davidson Cafe in Las Vegas will emerge having experienced fun and adventure in a polished, yet friendly atmosphere that links HD motorcycles with the freedom and ingenuity that have made America great."

OUT ON MAIN

COLUMBUS, OH

Design:
Chute Gerdeman, Columbus, OH

Photographer:
StudiOhio, Michael Houghton, Columbus, OH

Chute Gerdeman, a Columbus design firm, was challenged to create a warm and friendly eating/drinking oasis which would celebrate "the cultural and historical impact of gays and lesbians on American society." The target customers are educated and well traveled people who want more than just a meal, they want an experience.

The 3800 sq. ft. space is located in a building built in 1924 which though filled with unique features also presented many problems. The restaurant area needed to be redesigned to accommodate more diners and the memorabilia that would carry out the theme of the place. Where previously only 50 patrons could be seated, the new design can accommodate up to 125. On the alley side of the building, huge windows were added "to create an open,

This disease will be t
but not nearly all, th
and th
will s

and we will not go away.

The world only spins forward.
We will be citizens.

The time has come...
The Great

friendly environment" and glass walls replaced the original front entrance. The space is divided into a main bar/lounge area and three distinct dining spaces.

The bar area shares space with a coffee/espresso counter with pastries and a grand piano for live entertainment. Each of the dining areas—Celebration—Intimacy and Gathering—has its own ambiance and attitude.

Several wall murals by nationally recognized artists were commissioned for Out On Main and in addition there is an eclectic collection of gay and lesbian memorabilia on display. They range from valuable to fun to just plain fanciful.

Included are an Elton John costume, a Melissa Etheridge guitar, Speed-Os from Greg Louganis and even a tennis racket once owned by Martina Navratilova. Adding color and interest are original movie posters, classic Hollywood stills and old gay and lesbian pulp fiction novels.

The identity signage was designed to inspire the gay community to come "out" and celebrate. The letters O-U-T come to life with faces and movement while the color scheme is reflective of the rainbow of colors associated with the gay movement. Out On Main is a place that offers a sense of pride to the community.

THE BIG DOWNTOWN

CHICAGO, IL

Design:
Marve Cooper of Lieber Cooper Design,
Chicago, IL

Photographer:
Mark Ballogg, Steinkamp/Ballogg, Chicago, IL

"The toddlin' town" of the 1940s that Frank Sinatra sang about was the inspiration for the three restaurants in one located in the historic Palmer House in downtown Chicago. The "big downtown" is the fabled Loop district where entertainment, shopping and big business merge and this restaurant celebrates the fun-loving, culturally vibrant era of the '40s through "ingenious design and cleverly chosen artifacts."

The largest space, the dining room and bar area, is off the main entrance under the El tracks on Wabash Ave. Large scale models of the El trains that circled the Loop in the 1930s and 1940s cross the room at the ceiling line while the ceiling joists are bannered in period lettering with the names of the station stops. An overhead tunnel runs the length of the bar and the illuminated trains can

be seen entering and leaving the tunnel. A large TV screen, nearby, shows scenes from "Casablanca" and other films of that vintage. Colorful theater posters and playbills of plays of that period line the walls and a replica of the famous Chicago Theater marquee frames the open kitchen opposite the restaurant's streetside display windows. Over all of this a sound system plays music of the '30s and '40s.: jazz combos, big bands, and musical comedy favorites.

There are two additional long dining rooms. In one, tribute is paid to Chicago's jazz and blues heritage and the lyrics of "Home Sweet Chicago" are painted on the walls over framed photos of musical greats associated with Chicago. Wurlitzer-styled, satellite juke box controls are at each boothside and they showcase the music.

Chicago's theater life takes over in the other long dining room with theatrical publicity photos of countless, and sometimes nameless, actors, singers, and dancers. The design inspiration, here, is the interstate passenger rail travel and the booths have Pullman racks outfitted with antique leather luggage and vintage clothing.

The entry from the hotel is in the corridor that links the two rooms. The restaurant signage appears in the form of an immense, faux bronze, art deco fresco of an urban setting with a giant El train forcefully projecting outward.

CRAWDADDY BAYOU

WHEELER, IL

Design:
John Liautaud

Architect:
Jim Tinaglia

Photographer:
Mark Ballogg, Steinkampf/Ballog, Chicago, IL

Cajun Country came much closer to Chicago when Crawdaddy Bayou opened in Wheeler, IL. The brainchild and love child of the restaurant owner/designer, John Liautaud, the 344-seat restaurant and general store is filled with sights, sounds, smells and the tastes of bayou country. John Liautaud spent many years in the bayou country and comes from a New Orleans family. He was inspired to present an authentic Louisiana Acadian experience by combining down-home Cajun cuisine with the history of the bayou life in a custom-designed setting.

Diners enter through the General Store which is crammed full of Cajun and Creole gifts, foods and novelty

products presented in an "authentic" Cajun setting. The old barn wood that is used here and in the dining room came from old barns in Wisconsin that were razed. Old posters, signs, artifacts and antiques add to the clutter and "authenticity" of the General Store.

Beyond is the bar area where diners can enjoy specialty drinks, micro beers or indulge in food from two steam kettle of bayou seafood "boils" while being serenaded by live Zydeco or Canun music. The open kitchen, where the "boils" are prepared, provides another source of entertainment.

A lifelike bayou stretches from floor to ceiling and around the diner in the main dining room. Standing in the middle is a full grown cypress tree (cast in fiberglass from an original) with a spreading canopy of leaves and dripping Spanish moss. A 90 ft. by eight ft. high mural fills the perimeter wall. The mural was painted on canvas by Vincent Darby whose work is featured in many restaurants throughout Louisiana. Ben White, of White Light Design in Chicago, worked out a special lighting system of 28 natural colors to bathe the canvas and draw emphasis to the realism and depth of the mural. Diners can experience sunrise, midday or sundown in the bayou thanks to the lighting plan. To add to the realism, there is the sound of wildlife piped through the sound system: frogs, crickets and alligators. Through the taxidermy art of David Spires, guests can

see the alligators, raccoons, nutria, turtles and snakes amidst the bayou setting.

A private dining Bayou Shack, created out of the aforementioned barn lumber, is used for private and group dining. It is reached by crossing a swamp bridge beneath which some of the "stuffed" indigneous wildlife dwell. "One of the basics with the Cajun way of life is Southern hospitality: doors open and everyone feels welcome." Liautaud not only makes you welcome, he entertains and educates his guests as well.

FAMOUS DAVE'S

APPLETON, WI

Design:
Shea Architects, Inc., Minneapolis, MN
Ed Wilms

For Famous Dave's:
Ken Miller

AJ Signs:
Al Thomson

Photographer:
Stuart Lorenz Photographic Design Studios,
Minneapolis, MN

Each new Famous Dave's restaurant that opens is a collaboration between the Shea Architects design team and Famous Dave's own, in-house design and restaurant planning service. For the recently opened unit in Appleton, WI, Ed Wilms with Shea and Ken Miller of Famous Dave's together with their staffs and AJ Signs came up with the retro themed design shown here in a 5000 sq. ft. space.

The building exterior with its rough sawn cedar siding and wrap-around porch suggests a 1930s roadhouse. It was designed to recall those halcyon days and also to recom-

mend it to patrons looking for a fun and relaxing place to sip a lemonade or try the Famous Dave's Bar-B-Que. The strip of neon around the porch and the multicolored lights along with the new signage create the unique and distinctive look for this rapidly growing food operation.

There is a take-out counter in the waiting room which introduces the look of the restaurant. The rough sawn, pine paneled walls, the wood plank floors and the pitched wood ceiling with the barn-like trusses all carry through the "country style" architecture of Middle America in the 1930s. Signage, commercial posters and signs, framed photos of the past, artifacts and Americana memorabilia push and shove for every inch of displayable wall space and all together create a cacophony of visual stimuli and a sense of excitement. It is fun-for-all in this relaxed, easygoing, finger-lickin' food place.

In the main dining room, hoop back chairs are pulled up to the red and white, oil cloth covered tables. The open bar-b-que grill and rotisserie provide the mouthwatering show. The counter is highlighted with bright red painted brick below and a rusty, corrugated metal, shanty roof above the open-for-viewing space. Hanging from the angled ceiling amid the assorted drop lights are tires, hub caps, cans of oil and other atmospheric props.

Shea's team prepares the construction documents and supervises the construction of the Famous Dave's restaurants.

MERT'S HEART & SOUL

CHARLOTTE, NC

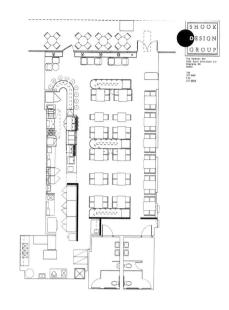

Design:
Shook Design Group, Charlotte, NC

Principal in charge:
Kevin E. Kelley, AIA:

Interior Design:
Mike Nicholls, AIA & Cicley Worrell

Graphic Design:
Steven Fenton & Ginger Riley

Photography:
Tim Buchman

To add an extra dollop of entertainment in dining to an area in Charlotte that was being revitalized and rehabbed into an Entertainment area, Mert's Heart & Soul restaurant was introduced. This small "soul food" cafe, designed by Shook Design Group, is now all set up in an uptown setting.

The designers conceptualized the name and logo . It is all about "Myrtle", a customer—now deceased—who frequented the client's former restaurant. This "real-life" link gave the restaurant owner an " historical and emotional tie with the customers." The 2235

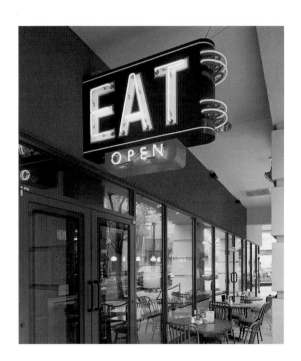

sq. ft. restaurant incorporates earth tones with bright accents and uses "alternative and urban materials to provide a diner-esque atmosphere with a touch of soul." The comfort and easy going attitude of an old diner is evident in the multicolored, checkered linoleum tile floor, the black formica counter edged in steel and the red naughehyde, vintage style bar stools. The mismatched tables and chairs add to the "attitude" of Mert's. The moderne curved dividers, at either end of the dining room, also suggest a bygone era. The lowered, blackened ceiling contributes to the charm and intimacy of the space.

Shooks Design Group was not only involved in the market positioning, concept development, and the architectural and interior design but with the graphics as well. They were responsible for everything from the logo to the outfits worn by the wait staff. Shook also commissioned local artists to decoupage, paint and contribute artwork to designated areas. The restaurant also houses folk art and an historical and nostalgic "time line" represented by photographs from private collections.

MEMPHIS SMOKE

ROYAL OAK, MI

Design:
JPRA Architects, Farmington Hills, MI

Dir. of Environmental Graphics:
Ron Rea:

Graphic Design:
Ron Rail

Architects:
Greg Tysowski / Ken Zawislak

Royal Oak is a suburb of Detroit that is rapidly being recognized as an entertainment center. JPRA Architects were challenged to create the image, the graphics and the store design for Memphis Smoke which features a style of barbequing that is unfamiliar to Detroit diners.. A great part of that challenge was to reorient five existing store fronts of 1920's vintage into an integrated and inviting single element on an important corner of this district.

The architects/designers approached the project with humor and the theme—"when pigs fly"— which became the graphic personification of Memphis Smoke. On the exterior there are canvas roof canopies with curlicues and flame motifs—also repeated in neon—and pig sculptures by Ron Brown of Renaissance Studio in Birmingham, MI. Metal signage wraps the cornice of the corner entrance and invites diners to enter and partake of " swine dining." The custom door pulls are shaped like pig's ribs.

Interior focal points include huge carved wood pigs: a chef pig, a guitar strumming pig, and a beer drinking and dancing pig. A $10,000 "pig clock" attracts attention by

sticking its tongue out to announce the hours. Continuing the porcine message are the light fixtures made of bisected BBQ barrels. Since the target audience varies from 20-year-olds up to diners in their sixties and seventies, and the restaurant does turn into a "blues club" after ten p.m., the interior design had to be flexible, adaptable and fun.

To create the open, casual setting, JPRA not only worked on the architecture and design layout—the color and material palette— but also assumed the responsibility to the theming, graphics and signage.

RED DEVIL BBQ

TORONTO, CANADA

Design:
Yabu Pushelberg, Toronto, ON

Photographer:
Volker Seding, Design Archives, Toronto, ON

The design firm , Yabu Pushelberg of Toronto, found its inspiration for the fun and flavorsome Red Devil BBQ restaurant in the roadside restaurants that dotted the sub-urban highways in the 1950s.

The name itself, Red Devil, also became a source for the imagery and the motifs that appear throughout. It all starts on the red brick exterior and the fantastic gate divider made up of wrought iron "pitch forks"—straight out of hell. The illuminated, drive-in style signage, out front, immediately sets the stage for a return to a bygone era and the road signs of those times.

Inside, the designers created a funky, down home atmos-phere that one associates with traditional Southern U.S.A. barbeque restaurants. The long bar with its ribbed steel front sits beneath a rough timber "portico." The back bar wall com-bines panels of galvanized corrugated metal with areas painted dark brown. Devilishly clever little red glass lanterns are suspended down between the raw wood beams.

Areas of rough, worn bricks add a visual texture to the space and Devil's pitch fork dividers separate the booths from one another. The flame-like lanterns also add to the hell-ish look of the restaurant. Most of the seating is real

"homey": mismatched chairs of vintage styles combined with "chrome set" residential type kitchen tables of the '50s. The diner style table top service—the dishes, cutlery, napkin dispensers, etc.—also contribute a patina of period to the setting.

Throughout, walls and ceilings are painted a deep reddish-brown and below the chair rail the walls are paneled with the corrugated galvanized metal. The floors are concrete with a clear matte finish and some areas are paved with flagstone. The oven, grill and rotisserie enclosures are of a " cultured stone" veneer and the millwork combines stained maple with stained oak. Graffiti on the walls, the ceiling-high fieldstone fireplace, pipes running across the ceiling, clusters of nostalgic pictures and shelves loaded with cans, tins, and jars— of a time now gone—all add to the "entertainment" of this friendly and fun restaurant of approximately 10,000 sq. ft.

FUEL PIZZA CAFE

CHARLOTTE, NC

Design:
Shook Design Group, Charlotte, NC

Project Architect:
Frank Quattrocchi

Interior Design:
Ann Erickson, IIDA

Project Architect:
George Price

Photographer:
Tim Buchman

Stephen Duncomb and Jeremy Wladis own and operate three restaurants in New York City. They wanted to open a "pizza-by-the-slice" cafe in Charlotte, NC and so approached the Shook Design Group, of Charlotte, looking for a novel, entertaining and unique design solution. Shown here is what they got: the Fuel Pizza Cafe.

The concept included the renovation and also restoration of a 1930s Pure Oil, Tudor-style, service station and then adapting it to the pizza-by-the-slice set-up. The name and concept, obviously, were derived from the architectural and former use of the structure and the site. The fun begins outside. It looks just like what it once was. Now, the covered service area, under the portico, serves as outdoor seating with communal tables. Inside, it is a trip back in time to the '30s. The interior is bright with light green, sharp red and sunny yellow gold colors, ocher colored formica topped tables bound in ridged aluminum and maple toned chairs. The exposed ceiling is true to the building's original use and "antique" cans, oil tins and such are lined up as decorative friezes, on shelves, over the tables and windows.

There are old posters, metal signs and other artifacts that relate to the gas/oil business of decades ago. The giant squares of red and black linoleum, set on the floor, complete the look of this fun and popular hangout.

RICK'S CAFE

RANDOLF, MA

Design:
Judd Brown Design, Warwick, RI

Photographer:
Warren Jagger Photography, Providence, RI

Rick's Cafe, like the "Cheers" bar of TV fame, could be a place where everybody knows your name—and where you feel very much at home. The client wanted to capture the entertainment value of an old fashioned, roadside grille—"for all ages." It had to be a destination which was familiar. The challenge for Judd Brown Design was to establish that unique feeling and environment in the midst of a suburban strip mall location.

The space had a high ceiling and an original floor plan that could be anything. Working within the space, the designers created a series of warm, worn, and comfortable individual spaces. One area was elevated three steps and "enclosed" to be a "roadside" structure that affords the diners in their brown naughehyde upholsters booths a sense of privacy and intimacy. According to Judd Brown, "The design captured the essence of a service station and a roadhouse with the excitement of an eclectic collection of treasures and souvenirs from the worldly adventures of a fictitious host named Rick."

Dark greens, browns, mustard yellows and sienna reds make up the deep, earthy and aged palette of the space. Beams, louvered shutters climbing up on an angle—to cut down the ceiling height— dropped metal lamp shades and walls so dark that they could be black, all combine to provide the desired, distressed background of Rick's Cafe. Assorted size rectangular shaped mirrors, in simple frames painted ocher or black, pattern the dark stained walls. Small ocher colored lamp shaded sconces add an extra touch of warmth as they light up the mustard colored fascia. The murals that appear are also subtle and subdued in color and they recall images of the 1930s and 1940s and especially of the movie "Casablanca" which featured the original "Rick's Place." The occasional potted palm, the spinning ceiling fans, the street markers, and the blowups of exotic hotel tags add to the fun and familiar feeling of the place. "The design created a world where the customer could be in the Casablanca Cafe on Rte. 66—without ever leaving his or her seat."

CHILE VERDE

GAHANNA, OH

Design:
Chute Gerdeman , Columbus, OH.

Photographer:
Michael Houghton, StudiOhio

Chile Verde, or green chili, not only is a popular pepper used to spice up Santa Fe dishes, it is also the name of the themed restaurant in Gahanna, OH designed by Chute Gerdeman. In keeping with the spirit of the cuisine, the design of the restaurant "reflects the beauty of New Mexico's outdoor architecture." What the designers created indoors is a series of out-of-doors patio settings under a sunset colored ceiling; "reminiscent of a cool summer evening in the southwestern desert."

The diner enters through an imported, authentically hand carved door into a waiting room furnished with rustic benches and scene setting cacti. Adjacent to the entry is a

small, serpentine shaped bar finished in weathered wood and acid washed bronze—to look like an antique Colonial Spanish buffet. Hanging over the bar are hand blown, indigo colored glass lamps.

"The key architectural element to the restaurant design is a massive Santa Fe style pergola with hand hewn cross members supported by hand carved corbels imported from New Mexico." Creating a celebratory mood are the strings of festive, multicolored lights and the chili peppers hanging over the tables. The stucco finished piers boast metal sconce lights with a motif of dancing Indians.

To emphasize the courtyard ambience, next to the pergola stands a cluster of fichus trees enhanced with twinkling lights. They help to visually differentiate the three distinct seating areas in addition to the aforementioned pergola. In one area, cozy candle-lit tables are set next to rustic, willow twig shutters while in another area guests can enjoy the warmth of a traditional, wood burning New

Mexico kiva. A curved wall, towards the rear of the restaurant, is painted turquoise/blue and it is decorated with niches filled with hand crafted artifacts and a built-in bench " to provide a more private seating area."

Throughout, the designers used a neutral toned adobe stucco on the walls accented with turquoise or lavender. A sienna washed concrete floor adds to the feeling of casual outdoors dining. The chairs and bar stools have a burnished metal finish, aniline dyed wood seats and cut out artwork that " captures the spirit of New Mexican metal artistry."

TAPIKA

NEW YORK, NY

Design:
Rockwell Architecture, New York, NY

Rockwell Architecture was commissioned to refurbish and reinterpret the character of a restaurant located on Eighth Ave. and W. 56th St. in New York. The owners, Peter and Penny Glazier, wanted a unique environment that would complement the southwestern cuisine: of chef David Walzog —and the result is shown here.

According to David Rockwell, the designer, "our design approach consisted of treating the 2400 sq. ft. space as two separate conditions: the inside or internal walls and the outside or perimeter walls." The "inside condition," which was defined by the former heavily paneled walls, was now sectionally ombre plastered in shadings of desert clay. The remaining wood, made of ash, was bleached, stained and wire brushed " to lighten and emphasize its texture." A fence motif is used to define the exterior perimeter and it

also incorporates hand painted draperies which shield patrons from the bright flashing lights out on the street. A seating platform, not only breaks up the dining hall look but divides the main dining room into three, intimate spaces. The added wainscoting was treated to match the walls and then branded with actual irons obtained in Texas.

The bar is located up front near the entrance and it has a leather-like upholstered front trimmed with nail heads. The wood bar top is outlined with a giant rounded edge. Lined up over the padded back bar are dozens of silhouette mounted cowboys riding off into the rich red/terra cotta sunset beyond. The deep, saucer-like, light fixtures are made of hammered metal and decorated with pierced Indian motifs. The uplighting illuminates the coffered ceiling while the light passing through the cut outs makes the giant fixtures stand out as decorative elements overhead. Small white mosaic tiles are laid in the floor and patterned into a grid by black tiles

In addition to the design of the restaurant, Rockwell also provided the custom designs for the furniture and fixtures as well as the lighting fixtures used in the space.

RED

NEW YORK, NY

Design:
Adamstein & Demetriou, Washington, DC
Olivia Demetriou and Theodore Adamstein
Project Architect: Ira Taitelman

Photographer:
Theodore Adamstein

For the Ark Co.'s new restaurant featuring Southwestern cuisine, the designers, Adamstein & Demetriou, created this " visually saturated" casual setting on Fulton St. in downtown New York. The concept focuses on the rich history of the American Southwest and freely celebrates and mixes the cultures of the Native Americans, Mexicans and the Americans. "Our intent was to create a space where one could feel the sensuality of Pueblo architecture and culture, overlaid with the transient, expansive and powerful architecture of the American west."

The designers have created bold architectural elements and forms with a variety of surfaces and textures to evoke that southwest sensibility: the hanging Red Rock

cliff, adobe walls that have been pierced and cut, and even massive, artist sculpted Chili peppers by Donna Reinsel that hang down from above. The sculpted interior space also provides " an exhilarating feeling of height" while the visual references are presented in a surrealistic manner. To suggest the hot sun, there are fiery wedges of orange glass hovering behind the rusty metal bar. The neglected "ghost towns" is alluded to by the wood logs hanging in a state of decay. The designers also added the natural rough red stone to " capture the sunset colors of the local cliffs and geology." The turquoise mosaic glass surfaces, by Rebecca

Cross, pay homage to the richness of the artwork and jewelry of the local artisans and craftspeople. Throughout, the designers used stained pine wood floors to further the look of the Old West as well as giant photo blowups of early photographs of Native Americans. The lighting fixtures that hang in the front part of the restaurant—near the bar—recall cactus plants and bleached animal horns.

The two levels of the restaurant are connected by a staircase in the rear of the space. On the mezzanine, the heavy logs , beams and timbers reinforce the deserted looks of ghost town constructions. A subtle colored upholstery fabric in reds, olives and ochers is used to cover the booth seat backs and that is complemented by the deep red vinyl seat covering. Throughout—the lighting is low-keyed and dramatic.

"Red was designed to be both whimsical and evocative, sensual and exciting."

WILDHORSE SALOON

LAKE BUENA VISTA, FL

Entertainment Design and Architecture:
Daroff Design, Inc.
DDI Architects P.C.
Philadelphia PA.

Principals in charge:
Karen Daroff
James Rappoport, AIA

Design Director:
Martin Komitzky

Project Manager:
Robert Hilton, AIA

Project Architect:
Keith Fallon, AIA

Design Team:
Martin Komitzky/Richard Marencic/
Philip Stinsor/Qi Wang

Graphic Design/Signage:
Glen Swantak/Simone Makoul

Client:
Gaylord Entertainment
Levy Restaurants

Photographer:
Elliott Kaufman, New York, NY

Like the name says—Wildhorse Saloon is a themed, western style restaurant/entertainment venue in Lake Buena Vista, Florida. This is a really big space that can accommodate about 1,000 guests. To top it off, Wildhorse Saloon also features live country music performances. These performances take place in 12,500 sq. ft. of club space and dance floor.

To energize the building's exterior and create a sense of anticipation and arrival, Daroff Design specified rusticated, distressed, corrugated metal siding, barn siding, and country billboards. Thundering, larger-than-life, three dimensional horses are seen stampeding over the trompe l'oeil mountains—to add visual excitement that animates the Pleasure Island entrance into the restaurant. The entry foyer opens into the "country fair" dance hall which is flanked by a pair of long bars. The bars have hammered copper tops and the fronts are covered with batten wood. Decorative metal horse cutouts on the fascia of the bar are backlit with theatrical lights, which are controlled by a

timer. The changing colors simulate the colors of the sky at dawn, at noon, and at twilight. To separate the bars from the dance floor, Daroff Design introduced rusticated hog wire and wood fences. Beyond the dance floor is the 25 ft. deep by 50 ft. wide stage, which is framed with the pitched roof barn motif. To illuminate the dance floor and the bar areas, theatrical lighting is used. The lights accentuate the bold, old colors of the "cast members" and the guests in their country-style outfits.

The retail store is 700 sq. ft. and is finished with recycled barn wood and a neutral palette. There is also a barn area and a general store. Accent colors of turquoise, cactus green and sun yellow reinforce the country theme, while the vintage store fixtures are integrated into the layout.

Wildhorse Saloon is a theatrical experience with a show thrown in for additional entertainment.

THE FLYING FISH CAFE

BOARDWALK RESORT,
WALT DISNEY
WORLD & RESORT
ORLANDO, FL

Architectural & Interior Design:
Dorf Associates Interior Design, Inc., New York, NY
Principal Designer/Project Architect: Martin E. Dorf

Design Team:
Ivonne E. Dorf/Michael Pandolfi/Allison Yi/
Colby Wong/Marina Hineman

For the Walt Disney Corporation:
Vice President Master Planning Architecture &
Design, Walt Disney Imagineering®:
Wing Chao

Sr. Development Mgr., Walt Disney Imagineering®:
Paul Katen

V.P. Food & Beverage, Walt Disney World:
Dieter Hannig

Lighting Design:
Martin E. Dorf, Bill Schwinghammer, Johnson
Schwinghammer, New York, NY

Photography:
Used by permission from Walt Disney
Enterprises, Inc

Inspired by Coney Island, the daredevil daring roller coasters of the 1920s, the Flying Fish Cafe in the Boardwalk Resort® at Walt Disney World in Florida recalls that time and place in its many entertaining features. "This restaurant embodies the spirit of Coney Island with abstract, dream-like shapes and forms such as the roller coaster, parachute jumps, fish bodies and tails, fish hook lights, and fish scales of all shapes and sizes." It all starts at the entry with the wave walls and fish hook and lily pad lights that all that follows is the realm of the Flying Fish—a famous roller coaster of that long ago time.

The excitement and the entertainment value is there—visually—in all the details. The fish scale columns that reappear throughout the space are finished with layers of automotive paint to "create depth and movement mimicking the look of a fish under water when sunlight is reflected off its body." The large banquettes that divide the space into intimate areas for dining are shaped like the seats on a whip ride. They are upholstered in a fabric that furthers the carnival-like imagery while also adding a dollop of energy and playfulness to the whole design. These seats are punctuated by the verticality of the "parachute jumps" which are constructed of structural steel clad with Lunsteed Metal's light etched pewter and brass. The gold leafed flying fish icons, hanging from the parachutes, are

highlights in this "fantastic adventureland." The balance of the seating is based on designs of the 1930s and 1940s while the tables have offset metal squares set within the light maple framing—to suggest a funhouse mirror look.

The Ferris wheel and roller coaster walls are trans-illuminated with fluorescent lamps to underscore the shapes and forms and also to enhance the sense of excitement which is also carried through in the murals art directed by Alix Beeney of Parker Blake of Castle Rock, CO. The mural, according to Martin Dorf, the principal designer of the project, captures "the absolute sense of joy, freedom, and wonderment combined with the mystery and excitement of Coney Island." The sky mural on the ceiling recreates the panorama of the outdoor amusement park.

The ceramic tiles, used on the floors, are mainly blues and greens and they are complemented by the salmon colored grout. Together they affect the illusion of the ocean floor. The materials were selected for their cost effectiveness, durability and ease of cleaning. The carpet carries through the feeling of waves and ocean currents with the Flying Fish logo appearing to swim upstream within the pattern of waves and sand.

At the Flying Fish Cafe light emanates from everywhere. Low voltage directional lamps in the ceiling spotlight each table. Resin light bulbs throughout the cafe are illuminated by fiber optics make the stars in the sky mural shine. Low voltage strip lighting illuminates the mural and creates a sense of layering on the funhouse wall. The flying fish torcheres with their uplights add the illusion of fish flying over them.

Everywhere you look in the Flying Fish Cafe there is a reminder of another time, another place and a way of life that was filled with wonderment. That place was Coney Island, with "its heightened sense of reality, its sense of joy, its mystique, with grotesque shapes and rides that swallowed you whole." Now-almost a century later-it is here to be enjoyed and savored-along with the delicious food-again.

CAFE SPIAGGA

CHICAGO, IL

Design:
Marve Cooper of Lieber Cooper Associates,
Chicago, IL

Photography:
Steinkamp/Ballog, Chicago, IL

For the contemporary Italian cuisine of Chef Bartolotta, the Levy Restaurants Corp. wanted a new, sophisticated and intimate look for the Cafe Spiagga. What Marve Cooper, now with Lieber Cooper Associates of Chicago produced was a setting that showcases modern Italian objects of art and design against a backdrop of pre-Renaissance frescoes inspired by the 15th century artist Andrea Mantegna. The mural reproductions were done on canvas by Simes Studio of Chicago and they are scenes from "La Camera degli Sposi" (the marriage chamber) in the Castello di San Giorgio in Mantua. In striking contrast to the early renaissance architectural and decorative features are the contemporary accents from the lighting fixtures to the table top accents. "These elements, coupled with art objects displayed in vitrines, are designed to showcase the work of modern Italian artists."

The space is distinguished by the bold checkered floor in charcoal and ocher tiles. The charcoal is repeated on the banquette seating along the walls and on the upholstery of the cherrywood chairs pulled up to the tables of the same

wood. The ocher color reappears on some of the walls between the applied murals that create the true ambience for the space.

According to Marve Cooper, "Our inspiration was to create a gallery setting for artwork and art objects from the 20th century, allowing our guests to experience a visual contrast of the very best in Italian art and design from two distinct eras. The excitement in Cafe Spiagga's cuisine and decor is in juxtaposition of the classic and contemporary. The artistic tension of the 15th century is really no different from that of the 20th century."

The Levy Restaurants Corp. intends to keep changing the exhibition of art objects displayed in Cafe Spiagga. Marve Cooper will serve as "curator" to ensure that as diners return on future visits they will find a new and visual entertainment experience that enhances the presentation and sampling of the cuisine.

RED SEA STAR

EILAT, ISRAEL

Interior Design:
Aqua Creations, Tel Aviv, Israel

Project Team:
Albi Serfaty & Yuval Levy

Architect:
Joseph Kiriary

Photographer:
Albi Serfaty

Often sea food restaurants will try to emulate an underwater ambiance but never before has a restaurant actually been constructed 20 ft. underwater. Red Sea Star, a most unique dining/entertainment facility, is located 100 ft. offshore of the resort city of Eilat in southern Israel. It is house in 3 welded steel tanks that are anchored in concrete and the large, diving-bell-like space is illuminated by 62 acrylic windows.

Ayala Serfaty of Aqua Creations is a noted designer of sea-inspired lighting fixtures and furniture. She was commissioned to rid the space of its cold, intimidating and somewhat claustrophobic ambiance. As she saw her task,

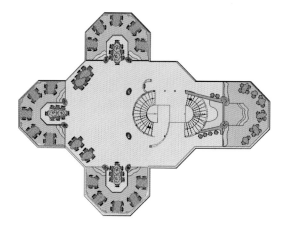

it was to turn "the interiors into a space that is about liquidity, floatation, tenderness and warmth." Ms. Serfaty says, "From the moment I began this project I was drawn to the colors of the sea." Her greatest obstacle, however, was the cold and chilling blue light that filled the sunken chambers and that cast sickly and unpleasant hues over everything and everyone. To overcome that, the designer arrived at a palette that was laden with rich, warm and glowing reds and oranges and those she applied lavishly to the assorted surfaces and furnishings.

The guests enter Red Sea Star at sea level-over a bridge-to the entry pavilion. Here is located a coffee bar, lounge and the kitchens. Patrons are led down two flights

via a spiral staircase to enter the bar and the main dining room. The walls are finished with plaster panels and the plaster finished ceiling is decorated with what look like giant sea pebbles. Actually they are constructed of acoustic melamine and covered with felt and serve as camouflage for the air vents as well as decorative accents. The designer treated the floor with transparent epoxy poured over sand to create the illusion of the floor of the sea. Epoxy was also used for the undulating and snaking shapes of the tabletops-all to evoke the sensation of "floating weightless on water." Continuing the undersea motifs are the coral reef-like shapes laser cut into the metal railings and the tentacle shaped bases of the bar stools.

Since the designer is known for her aqua-inspired lighting fixtures and columns, the silk constructions she has added to the design contribute to the overall feeling of a gentle movement in the underwater space. The soft, fluid shapes somehow detract from the industrial steel construction of the actual setting.

The unique restaurant has continuous entertainment presented by the living sea that surrounds it and that can be viewed through the many window openings. The fish and divers, separated from the diners only by the thickness of the acrylic windows, put on a show that varies from moment to moment and from visit to visit.

CAFE BRIACCO

BOSTON, MA

Design:
Bergmeyer Associates, Inc., Boston, MA

Principal in Charge & Project Architect:
Michael R. Davis, AIA

Design Team:
David Mayer / William Crowley, Jr.

Photographer:
Lucy Chen, Somerville, MA

This is the second downtown Boston location created by Bergmeyer Associates for Cafe Briacco. The goal, here, was to present the chef-owner's creative Mediterranean menu of pastas, pizzas, salads and hot entrees in a setting that is warm, contemporary and fun—and also sparkles with a modern Italian flavor

The signature design motif is the geometric pattern of bright red and sharp black aniline dye on natural pine that appears on the casework. Also, there are the dramatic wide stripes on the floor that relate to the structural piers of the office building in which the small cafe is located. The deep, rich red color appears on a focal wall in the rear dining area where the signature triangle shape is inlaid, also in red, on the small round metal tables that are used with the teal vinyl seated chairs . In the forward area, black, silver, gray and natural wood dominate for the walls, table tops and chairs. Dramatic lighting and handcrafted, artistic paint finishes are used "to add vibrancy and interest while controlling construction costs." The space is further distinguished by the curved stand-up dining counter and the cast plexiglass light fixtures.

ORO

TORONTO, CANADA

Design:
II X IV Design Associates, Toronto, ON

Photographer:
David Whittaker, Toronto, ON

Oro means "gold" in Italian and golden is the word that best describes the transformation that II X IV Design Associates accomplished in an old restaurant in downtown Toronto. The owners of the venerable restaurant were looking to reach out to a younger market but didn't want to lose its established but dwindling customer base. The miracle they wanted reproduced was a setting they had seen in Florence. However, without the centuries old building to work in and the towering 40 ft. ceiling the owners had so admired, the design team was able to capture the warm, golden glow of Florence and that city's architecture.

Full height windows were added to the facade for greater presence on the street and also to take advantage of the warm afternoon light. The new interior layout provides a sense of spaciousness as well as one of intimacy in a series of smaller, private dining rooms. Rather than discarding everything from the original restaurant, the designers kept the 1920's chests and side tables, the exquisite alabaster light fixtures, the elegant and comfort-

able chairs and several stained glass windows which were used in new situations.

One low curving wall includes banquette niches with "windows" to spaces beyond and other glazed partitions to create a sense of privacy while still allowing the flow of light. Gold leaf was used extensively to create the gilded illusion. Soft light from the alabaster fixtures that are hung between the ceiling arches reflect off the gold leaf pattern on the ceiling. In one of the private rooms, the face of the fireplace is gold leafed. Adding to the glow of the ambience are the rich finishes and materials such as brick, oak stained cedar, sandblasted cedar, figured anegre, the yellow granite bar top and the patterned upholstery fabrics.

The stone mosaic of the original entry now adorns the waiting lounge and the concrete floor is inlaid with a limestone brick pattern that becomes more subtle as it moves

away from, the walls. The same is true of the decorative ceiling treatment. Other elegant touches are the wrought iron stair rail and the ornate, sinuous curved wine rack behind the bar. Add the fresh flowers on the tables and the small table lamps in the banquette seating area and you have a wonderful, glowing gold, Florentine dining experience without ever visiting Italy.

VIA FORTUNA

MONTREAL, CANADA

Design:
Gervais Harding Associates, Montreal, QC

Principal:
Denis Gervais

Project Director / Designer:
Pierre Richard Robitaille

Intermediate Designer:
Sophie Lemabre

Project Director / Production Supervisor:
Ian M. Rors

Senior Designer:
James Lee

Architects:
Les Architectes Menkes, Montreal, QC

Photographer:
Yves Lefebvre

The design mandate for Gervais Harding Associates was to develop an Italian theme restaurant with a menu of pizzas and pastas that would appeal to a wide spectrum of patrons that come to the Casino de Montreal. The management specified about 150 seats (preferably at two seater tables for greater flexibility), an open kitchen, an eat-at bar, and service stations that could comfortably line up to 60 patrons.

The design concept was to create the feeling of an Italian village with its play of dark and light zones and piazzas. Thus, Gervais Harding's team created zones within the theme. The rotunda wraps around the monumental

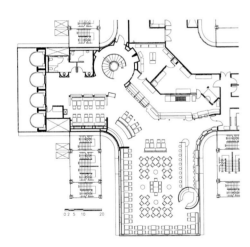

spiral staircase and this is where the "lineup" is found. Openings in the stone wall create a visual link to the open kitchen—a form of entertainment—for those who are waiting on line to be served. Each section or function of the open kitchen is treated differently: with awnings in the arcade and real foodstuffs on the shelves in the kitchen to enhance the market feeling.

The Petit Place (small piazza) is defined by a working fountain and visiting pigeons (molded in acrylic stone) and it is located in one of the "darker zones" in this make-believe village. There is seating here for about 24. An arcade separates the "town" from the open Grande Place which is in "full sun." Here, printed banners are suspended from the ceiling and illuminated to simulate sunlight filtered through foliage. While this piazza is open, the bar behind it is more "interior." The service consoles were inspired by street gazebos. In both dining rooms banquettes and low partitions, are used to facilitate the reorga-

nization of table groupings. At the end of the restaurant, sitting on a metal structure at eye level, is a scale model of an actual Italian island town which overlaps the actual horizon viewed through the window beyond it.

On the walls, the designers specified a combination of stone with terra cotta and painted stucco to convey the "old country" feeling. The arcade columns have vitrified tile bases and they are wrapped with hand painted canvases to create a Gothic-like colonnade. Ceramic tiles of assorted colors are used in a combination of patterns. Stone high-lighted with colorful cement tiles is used on the floor as a reflection of Mediterranean flooring. At night, when the lights are dimmed and the lamps take over, a whole new atmosphere is affected.

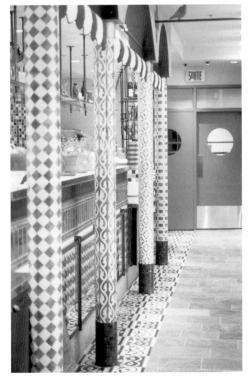

NAPLES 45

Design:
Frederick Brush Design Associates,
New Canaan, CT

Photographer:
Tim Lee / Lou Banna / David Brush

After an extensive tour of Naples, Nick Valenti, president of Restaurant Associates, decided that he wanted a restaurant that would reflect the authenticity in the food, the architecture, and the interior design that he had sampled and admired there. Frederick Brush was called in to realize his "dream."

For Frederick Brush that trip revealed the Neapolitans love of their past but also their acceptance of the simplicity and function of contemporary design." This is reflected in our sleekly designed tapas and drinking bar which is in contrast to the very large pizza table with its jumbo legs and intricate turnings."

In the restaurant, the warm white walls accent the "purity and softness" of the arches that appear throughout. The white wall tiles have deep bevels to create shadowed patterns and they are accented by diamond shaped terra cotta tiles. The terra cotta color, along with russet brown and yellow, is used as an accent color on walls where dec-

orative items are displayed and to paint some of the furniture. The custom booths and benches, in natural mahogany, were designed with both form and function in mind. Custom designed cushions are attached to the backs of the booths and benches for added color and comfort. The simple iron bases that support the mahogany table tops are also "a reflection of the marriage between the old and the new." Of special interest are the wall sconces that appear on the four corners of each column. "Looking like contemporary torches, the simplicity of the shape of the fixture against the whimsey of the flame-like glass panels make them truly unique". These sconces provide the general light of the restaurant. Secondary track lighting, made of black iron tubing suspended down on thin rods, undulate

across the ceiling and highlight key items or spaces. The floor design, which according to the designer is "playful and almost childlike," consists of free formed shapes of color that flow throughout the restaurant.

Focal to the overall design and a source of entertainment are the three wood burning pizza ovens named after the Italian volcanoes: Stromboli, Etna and Vesuvius. The giant pizza table, previously mentioned, is another attrac-

tion with its lower shelves stacked with sacks of Neapolitan flour that is used to make the pizza. The wall mounted pizza shovels, to the right of the ovens, are replicas of awards given by the guild in Italy.

The restaurant has attracted many young professionals in their '20s and '30s who come in groups for lunch and for after-work socializing—on pizzas.

SPEZZO RESTAURANT

TORONTO, CANADA

Design:
Hirschberg Design Group, Toronto, ON
Martin Hirschberg

Photographer:
Richard Johnson, Interior Images

FLOOR PLAN

Spezzo projects an image of an inviting Italian restaurant with an upscale menu while at the same time it offers a relaxed, comfortable and non-intimidating atmosphere. As designed by the Hirschberg Design Group of Toronto, one is immediately aware of the lit candles, the warm colors, rich textures and the sensual ironwork that flows throughout.

To produce a feeling of movement and still maintain a sense of sophistication, the designers remodeled the restaurant to place the emphasis on the food—and the preparation of the food. The kitchen area was opened up and pulled back to accommodate a pizza oven as well as dessert and antipasti facilities. A large presentation table was brought forward and a chef's table for patrons (by reservation only) has a central location within this area.

This opening up of the kitchen not only provides a more open and spacious feeling but makes the diners feel involved in the theater that is going on all around them.

The original L-shaped space was altered by the removal of the center wall and thus the bar area now is also more open. By adding a curved nook to the middle of the dining room, some intimate dining spaces were created. To keep these spaces from "closing in," curved, low height partitions with columns supporting a small bulkhead above were used to affect interesting sections or spaces. Customers in the rear area can still see through to the bar.

To create the inviting, country style ambience, warm textures and colors were selected. A rustic feeling was created by the faux finishes in neutral taupe, rust and olive green. Adding to the earthiness of the palette is the rich cherrywood and the dark, slate-like floors. Abstracted curves of organic shaped wrought iron flow throughout and forged metal chairs were chosen to coordinate. Booths were added for intimacy but they also introduce soft, sound absorbing finishes. Curved bench seating was added for the same reason. Live jazz, in the lounge/bar, makes another entertaining reason for dining at Spezzo.

PROVENCE

WASHINGTON, DC

Design:
Adamstein & Demetriou, Architects,
Washington, DC

Photography:
Theodore Adamstein

The "West End" district of Washington, DC is located between Georgetown and Downtown. The designers, Adamstein & Demetriou, attempted to recreate the ambience of Provence in the new restaurant of the same name which is located in this area. The design concept was planned to complement the menu which is a product of the chef Yannick Cam and the owner Savino Recine. The restaurant specializes in the regional cooking of Southern France "where rustic cuisine and high cooking meet."

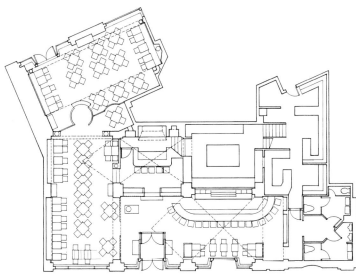

A wood burning grill greets the diners as they enter into Provence and much of the tantalizing aroma arises from the aromatic herbs used in the cooking: rosemary, lavender, fennel, anise and thyme. The interior is warm and inviting and the architects/designers have filled the space with the textures and colors that enhance the earthy atmosphere. The limestone walls, both real and faux finished (Lenore Winters) are equipped with custom designed wall sconces and the floors are a combination of terra cotta tiles and stone pavers. The banquettes are covered with tapestry-like fabrics and combined with other atmospheric details such as French tile counters, antique Provincial furniture, architectural fragments and specially designed and crafted ironwork. The vaulted ceilings not only provide a feeling of intimacy but help to define the areas within the dining room.

MEDITERRANEO

GREENWICH, CT

Design:
Haverson Architecture & Design, Greenwich, CT

Photographer:
Paul Warchol, New York, NY

All aboard for a cruise on the Mediterranean: blue skies, turquoise water, golden sun and sand. With that concept in mind, Haverson Architecture & Design transformed a former luncheonette into a shipshape, seagoing "experience" for 70 fortunate "passengers"/diners. The yacht-like environment is an authentic reflection of the modern sailor's dream which imaginatively utilizes the rigging, decking, hardware and materials found aboard a 65 ft. boat. Suggestions of the sea and sailing in primary colors are combined with the warm, sun drenched colors of the Mediterranean and blend with touches of the ports of call on which the menu is based.

White French doors and a canopy wrap around the facade. The chamfered entry is covered by a traditionally European metal and glass marquee. Inside, the actual

working kitchen is the star attraction of the dining room. An angled, bowed bar with a patterned stainless steel top and mahogany bullnose edge serves as a divider. Taller banquette tops affect warm and private dining niches in the corners while the floor is filled with custom tables and chairs made of teak and aluminum. Authentic booms support the wavy banquette tops. The teak and holly floor is constructed to look like the deck of a modern yacht. On the ceiling, an oversized, antique mural—framed by a continuous cornice—depicts the Cote d'Azur .

According to the designers, the lighting in a space so small is critical. The primary source of illumination is from a low voltage cable system strung from each side of the ceiling cove . This backsplashes light onto the nautical chart mural mentioned above. The cove itself contains fluorescent fixtures with amber gels and light baffles. This adds a warm, sunny glow to the edge of the mural. The lighting points up the tables' surfaces and accents the rope columns and sailing artifacts that enrich the space. A continuous soffit of recessed fixtures illuminates the bar surface and a quartz light strip washes the face of the bar with its gold leaf signage. Nautical themed, surface mounted, incandescent fixtures are centered in the bays of the lowered ceiling around the mural.

OPA

TORONTO, CANADA

Design:
II X LV Design Associates, Toronto, ON

Photographer:
David Whitaker

OPA! Is to Greeks what OLE! Is to Spaniards. It is a joyous exclamation and Opa, a Greek inspired dining experience is a joyous and interesting place to visit. The designers, II X IV Design Associates chose an image of a standing man of Naxos (the Greek island believed to be the home of Dionysus—the god of wine making) along with a modified Greek key or meander motif to tie the space together.

The color scheme "evokes the sparkling seas and glowing sands of the region." The walls are faux finished in soft yellow "sand" while the carpet and upholstery pick up all the shades of the ocean vista—from turquoise to purple. The principal area is dominated by a massive bar with ceramic and glass mosaic top above a stained plywood

base which is inlaid with the recurring meander motif. A
tall sand sculpture, like the six ft. one at the host's station,
pierces the bar top and becomes a fountain which directs a
trickling stream through a trough all along the bar top. The
arc of the bar is paralleled by a dining bar and also the
colonnade which delineates the dining lounge. Here, the
blue/green painted columns stand on the bar's concrete
floor which simulates wavelike forms, outlined in black,
that eventually merges with the turquoise/purple carpeting
of the dining area.

Table tops and drink rails are made of stained plywood
inlaid with the Greek key pattern which is also used for the
metalwork of the stair rail and the bright yellow welting on
the bar stools, the chairs, sofas and banquettes. The upholstery fabrics are aptly named "deep seas" and "sunlight."
Behind a built-in banquette, sandblasted glass reveals wine
bottles on display—lit from behind. Sandblasted glass is
also used for the custom fixtures that are mounted on the
columns. Wall sconces and pendant fixtures are strategically placed atop highlight tables and bars.

"The design inspiration was from ancient Greece, but
the result is a bright, lively and thoroughly modern addition to Danforth Ave.'s Restaurant Row."

COCO LOCO

WASHINGTON, DC

Design:
Adamstein & Demetriou , Washington, DC

Photographer:
Max McKenzie

A Brazilian themed restaurant can be a rich and wonderful mix of cultural and architectural styles. In addition to the flamboyant "carnivale" celebration associated with Rio, the designers/architects Adamstein & Demetriou could select from Portuguese, Baroque, Amazonian and Modern themes and styles as well. Coco Loco, in Washington, DC is a lively, medium-priced restaurant that features Brazilian rotisseried meats, seafood, antipasti and tapas in a setting that is casual, cool, exciting and exotic.

The designers opted for a neutral palette for the "envelop" of the restaurant and used simple and austere Portuguese elements such as stucco walls, terra cotta floors, rich wood finishes and ironwork details. The more "carnivale" design elements were fitted into this "envelop" like the amorphic columns that actually transfigure existing structural supports. Each has a different saturated color which dominates its space. The canopy of the bar curves upwards, echoing the line of a bull's horns. "The

entire restaurant is overlaid with a grid of beams providing a Cartesian grid against which the different zones and free forms can break away."

The front part of the restaurant is like an outdoor veranda with a vaulted ceiling, terra cotta pavers on the floor and furnished with wicker chairs and tables decoratively painted with tropical foliage. Ceiling fans, potted palms and broken tile mosaic accents add to the ambience as does the large mural of fruit pickers on a sunny day that serves as a focal point. The palette in the main dining room is richer and deeper with red mahogany tables and chairs and a procession of columns and colorful carnivale

lanterns. The focal point here is the unique antipasti table with the sneeze guard constructed of twisted and snaked, hand forged iron with a triangular mirror to reflect the food presented below. The broken tile mosaic that clads the open kitchen counters is an interpretation of the tropical theme used on the banquette upholstery fabric. As a backdrop for late night dancing, there is an abstract mural that suggests a steamy night in Rio. Towards the rear of the dining room one finds the primitive forms found in nature that throbs through the Amazon: a series of iron spears are draped overhead with custom bamboo reed pendants.

TAZA

CHICAGO, IL

Design:
Lieber Cooper Associates, Chicago, IL

Design Team:
Principal: Marve Cooper
Sr. Project Designer: Pablo Mosquera
Designer: Gina Hesler

Graphics:
Jim Lange , Jim Lange Design

Mosaic Tile Design:
Luis Encarnado

Photography:
Mark Ballogg , Steinkamp / Ballogg , Chicago, IL

The company, Al-Tazaj Barbeque Chicken, wanted to create a signature restaurant design that would quickly establish Taza as a premier, quick-service place—with a unique twist. This isn't just "barbecued chicken" but it is barbecued chicken with an exotic extra. The charcoal grilled rotisserie chicken is made on the premises—in view of the diners— and served on "made-from-scratch" pita breads baked in pit ovens also on the premises. Together, the chicken and the pitas assault the incoming patrons with their wonderful aromas.

The design firm, Lieber Cooper Associates, responded to the design challenge with the prototype shown here.

The design expresses a "global, fun, contemporary theme which has public appeal both nationally and internationally." The bold colors and abstract art provide a synergy which sets the tone for the space. These amusing abstract colors and forms are translated into volumes and shapes that give the restaurant its unique look.

Throughout, entertainment is provided with visual and audio stimulants and one of the focal highlights is the mural over the open and action filled kitchen where diners can watch the rotisserie process as well as the preparation and presentation of their individual orders. Other audio/visual stimuli are the TV monitors that broadcast world news. This restaurant is located only a block away from the Chicago Art Institute which provides Taza with a large international clientele as well as the young professionals that pour out of the office buildings for lunch and snacks.

SUSANNA FOO

PHILADELPHIA, PA

Design:
Marguerite Rodgers Ltd., Philadelphia, PA

Photographer:
Matt Wargo

The scents of green reed plants, small trees and flowers combined with the sound of dripping water sets the relaxing ambiance for the 23 ft by 105 ft Susanna Foo Chinese restaurant in Philadelphia. Located in an upscale shopping area, the design by Marguerite Rodgers makes use of mirrors and water to "reflect and refract light from unrevealed sources." With a palette of earthtones, wood, stone and glass, the space takes on "the peaceful mood of natural beauty and serenity."

The space, originally a dark and oppressive steakhouse, was completely gutted. Custom booths and banquettes were designed to maximize seating and provide

comfort in the long and narrow space. The earthy palette appears in the quiet, patterned, low pile carpet laid on the floor and a dozen silk lanterns create "a glowing necklace of light" that encircles the room.

The focal point in the restaurant is the private dining area which can accommodate 14 guests. This is The Empress Den and it is located at the end of the dining room and it is "shrouded by sheer, luminous curtains and richly decorated with intricate wood grill work, upholstered walls and a large, glowing lantern."

The ivory toned walls not only help to open up the space but they seem to emanate an opalescent hue. Diffused natural light streams through the plantation-style shutters on the windows during the daylight hours. At night, the soft glow of the lanterns combined with the subtle lighting plan takes over and integrates the architecture.

Working closely with the chef/owner, Susanna Foo and her husband, Marguerite Rodgers incorporated Chinese art and artifacts, calligraphy, scrolls, textiles and furniture from the owners' extensive personal collection into the decor of the room.

BUDDAKAN

PHILADELPHIA, PA

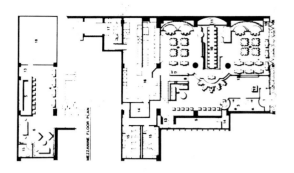

Design:
Chris Smith of CMS Design and
Stephen Starr: owner of Buddakan
Owen Kamihara: assisting.

Photographer:
Jim Graham, Philadelphia, PA

Located in Old Town, on Chestnut St. in Philadelphia is this super elegant, super handsome restaurant featuring modern Asian cuisine. The-170-seat restaurant was conceived and designed by Stephen Starr who owns it and he collaborated with Chris Smith of CMS Design. The source of inspiration was Wolfgang Puck's Chinois on Main and Oba Chine in Los Angeles. Also, the design pays homage to the design work of Phillipe Starck. "As soon as you enter Buddakan it transports you to a magical new world. You

could be in an exotic Asian land or in a sophisticated metropolis like New York City or Hong Kong," says Mr. Starr

Guests enter through ribbon striped mahogany doors into the reception area where a waterfall, Japanese river stones and a boulder are artfully arranged. A computerized reservation and table management system ensures efficiency and service for the guests. Inside, the color is white! Walls are draped in white fabric "exuding a heavenly quality" as soft lighting emanates from behind the fabric. The focal

point in the 100-seat dining room with the 20 ft. ceiling is the ten ft. tall, gold leafed Buddah. The floors are cherry wood and the furniture is Starck-like with curved high backed banquettes and chairs. The chairs, "abstract and surreal in design," feature photographic images of people's faces hand painted on their backs Many of the "faces" portrayed are noted local Philadelphians. The social center of the dining room is the 22-seat, onyx topped community table where guests can mingle while dining. "Whether you

are single, come as a couple, or as a group—the community table is a fun way to meet new people," says Stephen Starr.

Behind the backlit, golden onyx bar, large panels of sheer white fabric are draped from the ceiling. Twinkling lights, behind the curtain, suggest a "wall of soft candle lights." A 35-seat mezzanine area overlooks the airy dining space. Plush white chaise lounges provide the seating and a second bar serves exotic and unusual drinks as well as an extensive list of sake. Here, too, the walls are fabric covered and " glimmers with an elegant, celestial luminescence." In

addition, weather permitting, there is a 20-seat outdoor cafe which is set up with comfortable sofas and lounge chairs.

A refined sound system plays current music personally selected by Starr to complement the mood—day or night. "Following the tradition of Asian cultures, Buddakan provides a family-style dining experience by offering plentiful portions designed to be shared.

"It is Buddakan's suggestion that you pass our plates among your friends and companions and embrace this custom as well".

TOMMY TANG'S

PASADENA, CA

Design:
R.W. Smith & Co., San Diego, CA
Karen Montcrief

Photography:
Milroy/ McAleer

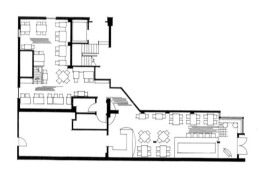

Designed as a backdrop for the well known chef/owner, Tommy Tang, the restaurant occupies an old historic building on Colorado Blvd. In the trendy, redeveloped, entertainment/ retail section of old Pasadena. The original storefront and arched grillwork over the door has been retained.

Inside, the columns are also original and they were uncovered during the renovation. The designers have chosen to treat them as made of natural iron. The entry floor is finished in porcelain tiles of black, gold, gray and cream while the pecan planks, used on the main floor, have been lightly distressed and finished. The interior is contemporary in feeling with natural contrasting materials and a subdued color palette of subtle Asian tones. The walls combine areas of old warm brick that was long hidden under plaster. Also revealed during the renovation were areas faux finished in taupe gray highlighted with gold. Black lacquered accents and the fine black metal furniture add to the delicate Asian look.

Gold beaded pendants hang over the bar which is backed up by the textured worn brick walls. They pick up the gold accent color "as well as enhance the concept of natural materials, with their free form shapes."

The cuisine is contemporary Thai food with an emphasis on spectacular presentation. Adding to the ever changing scene is the rotating art exhibit which features the work of contemporary local artists.

MIZU 212

LOS ANGELES, CA

Design:
AHA Architects, Los Angeles, CA
Amin Atlaschi & Russell Hatfield

Photographer:
Paul Bielenberg

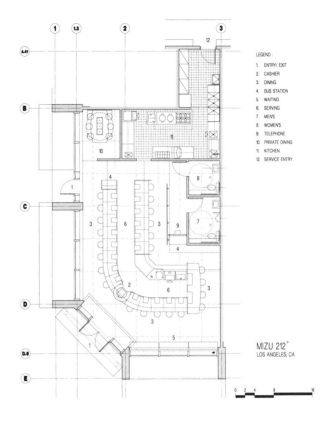

LEGEND :
1. ENTRY/ EXIT
2. CASHER
3. DINING
4. BUS STATION
5. WAITING
6. SERVING
7. MEN'S
8. WOMEN'S
9. TELEPHONE
10. PRIVATE DINING
11. KITCHEN
12. SERVICE ENTRY

MIZU 212°
LOS ANGELES, CA

The program for Atlaschi + Hatfield (AHA) Architects of Los Angeles was to create a definitive look for a 1600 sq. ft. Japanese Shabu Shabu restaurant in a new Japanese themed retail center in West Los Angeles. The design had to reinforce Shabu Shabu's fun approach to informal dining and also had to attract a more sophisticated young professional and college student clientele. The presentation had to be amicable and easy for the non-Asian diners while still staying true to the Asian roots of the concept. For the uninitiated, this is to be an alternative to the Sushi restaurants already in the neighborhood.

The design solution defines Japanese aesthetic sensibilities in a progressive manner with textures, colors and finishes still the primary design elements. Integrated with the Japanese ideal of restraint is the Western concept of extravagance. Since the steam that rises from the boiling water on the hot plates at each dining station needs to be vented out, the designers used the necessary exhausts as a design opportunity rather than a liability. " The resulting hood construction grants the space its shape, flow and

scale." The small but high space is carved into distinctive zones of intimate scale for diners who are all seated at the counter. A small private dining room (for two to six) is separated from the main room. A custom designed screen of sand blasted aluminum and diffused ribbed plastic panels serves as a semitransparent separation between the restrooms and the dining area. The lighting scheme is multilayered and flexible to set the mood depending upon the time of day or night.

MONSOON RESTAURANT

LEBANON, NH

Architect / Designers:
Paul Lukez Architecture and Arrowstreet
Associates, Architects

Artist:
Roger Chudzick

Color & Material Palette:
Gail Lindsay

Interior Photography:
Greg Premru

The entertainment feature that the architects/designers emphasized in the 8000 sq. ft. restaurant is the culture and tradition of open kitchen cooking found in Asia. Since Monsoon's menu is Pan-Asian, the designers, through the use of contemporary materials and technology combined with a wide range of Asian architectural elements created a setting that provides "a multi faceted dining environment" that is enriched by the contributions of artists and craftspeople.

The open kitchen is on view beneath the tilted canopy that is set over the grill. This immediately defines the focal point of the restaurant. A stainless steel counter wraps around the grill and serves as well as a display surface for the fresh vegetables and other ingredients that are used in the preparation of the food. The seating is oriented around the kitchen—"as though it were a theater" and the preparation and presentation the star attraction. The main dining room can seat up to 150 and an additional 50 can be seated at the bar and on the patio.

The architects/designers have selected elements from several East Asian cultures to affect the setting. The milky screens above the cook-line recall Japanese shoji screens and bamboo columns, wrapped and bound in copper ties, also find their origin in the orient's use of materials and joinery. The cloud-like ceiling system consists of wire mesh panels "reminiscent of traditional screens found in East Asian design." The end result, Monsoon, is an example of a unique collaboration between the owners, designers, craftspeople and artists. The large slate was mined by the artists and the knot of reed-like iron rods was locally forged. Local artists and the architects conceived the two sculptures.

STIR CRAZY

CHICAGO, IL

Design:
Marve Cooper of Lieber Cooper Associates ,
Chicago, IL

Photographer:
Mark Ballogg, Steinkamp Ballogg, Chicago, IL

What could be more entertaining than being in the heart of an Asian marketplace surrounded by a varied and colorful selection of meats, vegetables, noodles, sauces and condiments and then watching the high energy, exciting and unbelievable dexterity of the wok chefs cooking up your own special selection and mixture of ingredients? As of now, a visit to Stir Crazy, located in an upscale mall in the Chicago area, is as close as it gets to the real thing.

A sculptured awning, somewhat like a Japanese kite, bows around the building's corner. The entry location is emphasized by the traditional Japanese shoji screened

window. Designed by Marve Cooper, Stir Crazy offers customers fresh and light versions of Asian cuisine in an energetic and interactive dining environment. The setting not only explains the stir fry concept of cooking to a highly diverse audience, but also reflects the restaurant's combination of traditional wok cooking with a creative contemporary, Asian inspired, cuisine. The open kitchen and all the activity going on is the center stage of the design and surrounding it are Asian artifacts and weathered bamboo fencing to " establish the restaurant's authenticity."

The dining room is comfortable and relaxing in contrast to the exuberance exhibited in the kitchen. Natural materials and exotic painted textures create a backdrop for the playfully layered decor. The Pan Asian theme culminates in a wrought iron dragon head that ends the decorative serpentine ironwork railing that meanders from booth

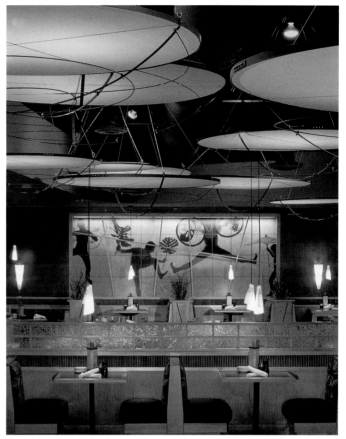

to booth. A recurring fun motif is the giant wood and iron chopsticks that appear inside and outside of Stir Crazy. Custom, cloud-like lighting fixtures are suspended throughout the space to cast a soft amber hue that makes everything it touches glow.

Stir Crazy is upbeat and contemporary. It is comfortable for a broad spectrum of dining occasions and offers the flavors and freshness of the Pan Asian cuisine combined with a keen sense of style and entertainment.

FIRE & ICE

CAMBRIDGE, MA

Design :
Prellwitz / Chilinski Associates, Inc.
Cambridge, MA

Principal in Charge:
David Chilinski

Project Architect:
Mark Conner

Project Designer:
Chris Brown

Interior Design:
Susan Greco

Photographer:
Steve Rosenthal

At Fire & Ice the diners can create and participate in the entertainment of dining. In the interactive setting by Prellwitz / Chilinski Associates of Cambridge for the Round Grille Co, Guests are invited to select their own ingredients from the fresh victuals presented before them and then watch them being cooked over a grill. "The fun and entertainment is not an add-on or an overlay to the food service. The concept is a very visual, engaging process that blends the drama of an open kitchen with a virtually limitless variety of superb, healthy meals."

Fire & Ice is a play between the cool, calm and relaxed bar area up front and the fiery hot grill and the dining room beyond. "Tumbling" wall panels in cool colors line the stairs leading from the street to the restaurant's sub-street location. In the bar area "Ice" is the dominant theme and it is executed in a variety of dark blues and greens in a fluid flow of panels. "Fire" takes over at the grill and the design elements radiate out like flames in red and gold in angular shapes and forms. "The layered vocabulary of forms creates a collage effect." The diners are directed to the "market" area where they may choose from the assorted meats, sea foods, vegetables, fruits, pastas and sauces. They then bring their selection to a dramatic round grill

centrally located in the dining room where with flair and pizzazz the chefs cook the food. They provide the visual entertainment. To bring all this off effectively, the designers also had to design the space with a limited budget. Sections of plywood, in a harlequin pattern, cover the walls and also serve as dividers. Ordinary table lamps become signature design elements when turned upside down and finished off with funky shades. Multicolored light bulbs were used to artfully light up the walls, columns and dividers. Special plastic trays were designed to serve as

"palettes" for the patrons' culinary creations.

"The energy of the concept combined with the lighting and the colors puts people in the mood to do something 'experimental,'" says David Chilinski.

The fun, colorful and impressive 7700 sq. ft. restaurant/bar can seat 190 indoors and another 50 in the outdoor courtyard. The designers were involved in the total project from its inception: site selection, graphic design, restaurant design, graphics, menu—and even the name.

ALCATRAZ BREWERY

TEMPE, AZ

Design:
Engstrom Design Group, San Rafael, CA
Jennifer Johnson, AIA / Katy Hallal, AIA /
Barbara Hofling

Photographer:
Andrew Kramer

The 400-seat restaurant/ brewery designed by Engstrom Design Group brings the sights and sounds of San Francisco Bay and the notorious "Rock" to Tempe, AZ. The brew pub is located in the new Arizona Mills development. The interior storefront is framed by jail bar canopies and laser-cut figurines of men on a chain gang. From outside the mall, one can see an institutional Federal era storefront with quoined stone and pilasters. The signage is located atop a 40 ft. replica of a water tower which in actuality stores the grain used to make the beer in the brewery.

The 13,000 sq. ft. space boasts of a twenty six foot vertical height and four woven steel sentry towers dominate the soaring space of the dining area. Each tower is guarded by a mannequin dressed as a prison guard. A free standing, 24 ft. tall replica of the Golden Gate Bridge spans the bar while painted murals depict cell block rows and other scenes of the Bay area. Overhead catwalks and an

actual walk-in jail cell add to the experience—" a scintillating interpretation of what it is like to do time in Hellcatraz". To complete the illusion, search light beams, from a stucco finished "lighthouse" play over the patrons and in the background one can hear the sound of seals, foghorns and cable car bells clanging.

The brewing process, in a linear progression from the entry, is on view to entertain and divert the patrons. After passing under the grain silo and the mill room, patrons see the brewing room where the beer simmers in copper and steel vats. Twelve ft. tall, stainless steel fermentation tanks line the way into the restaurant and bar. Seven, hand-crafted beers are brewed on site.

GORDON BIERSCH BREWERY / RESTAURANT

TEMPE, AZ

Design:
Allied Architecture & Design , San Francisco, CA
Mike Chen / Roddy Creedon / Kotting Luo / Mark
Schwettmann

Photography:
Property of Gordon Biersch Brewery

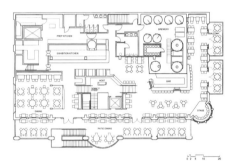

Located on the second floor of a building in the downtown area of the college town of Tempe, the design of this Gordon Biersch Brewery/Restaurant posed several problems for the designers, Allied Architecture & Design of San Francisco. A primary concern was making the entrance visible since the actual restaurant is 20 ft. above the sidewalk. To address this, a small intermediate floor was established below the main level. Here was placed the host area, retail displays and the beer stein lockers for "the regulars." A suspended plane of metallic ceiling panels serves to punctuate this point of entry into the space as well as serve as a buffer that separates the bar activity from the quieter, more formal dining area.

As in other Gordon Biersch breweries/pubs designed by AAD, signature mustard yellow tiles weave through both the brewery and the exhibition kitchen—highlighting the wood burning oven and rotisserie. The bar has mahogany paneled sides and a polished Indian red granite top. In contrast to all these glossy surfaces, the building's exposed brick walls are on view around the perimeter of the space. The traditional detailing of the mahogany millwork contrasts with the modern form of the space itself.

The brewery "is a visual and spatial focal point" in the design. Enclosed in glass from floor to ceiling, the brewery's 17 ft. tall tanks and the 60 barrel brewhouse set directly behind the bar are visible from almost every part of the restaurant.

LOCAL COLOR BREWING CO.

NOVI. MI

Design:
JPRA Architects, Farmington Hills, MI

Photographer:
Laszlo Regos Photography

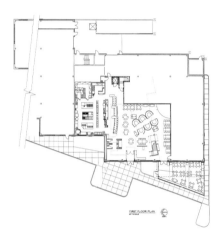

FIRST FLOOR PLAN

Main St, Novi is the fast growing suburb's creation of a "downtown" destination for dining, entertainment and shopping. The 20,000 sq. ft. brew pub/restaurant is set in the second phase of that entertainment destination development. The design concept, according to the designers at JPRA Architects, was to unite the technology of beer making with agriculture and the growing process.

Throughout the pub design there are strong references to nature such as trees, stone and a palette of warm earth tones. These are accented by geometric shapes of brilliant color. The four level structure has a bar on the first and third levels while the second floor contains sheltered booths and intimate seating . Up on the third floor there is additional space for mingling and informal gatherings with lounge chairs and sofas for seating. It is here that the local "color" is truly evident. There are bold, colorfilled paintings on the walls, on the ceiling and even some of the uphol-

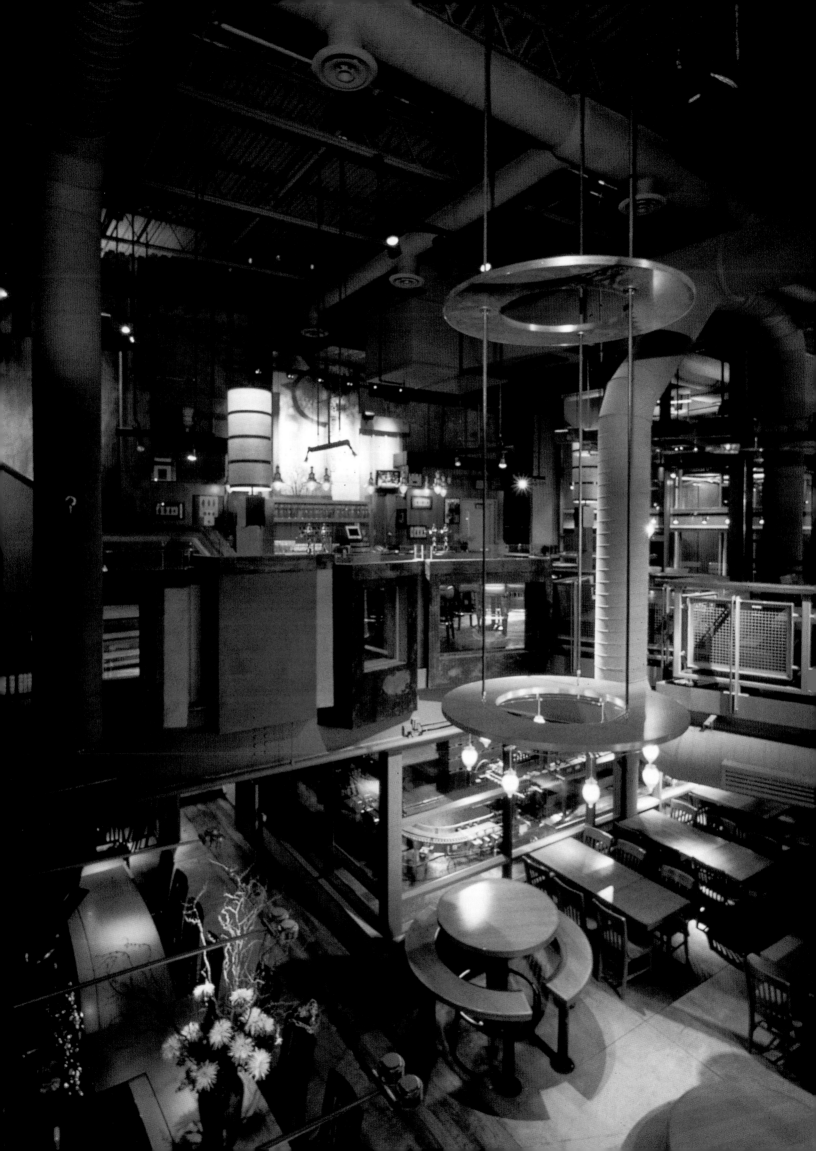

stery used to cover the soft seating picks up patterns and colors that are exotic as well as local. From each level, the patron can see into the brewing area. The bottling line and the more arcane process of beer making becomes part of the attraction and entertainment value of the brew pub.

The four seasons of the year are projected through the use of color and the overall space combines the old and the new in a simple and pleasing way. In the same way, the space and the design is urban and yet comfortable—"a friendly place to enjoy friends, food and drink." In a reference to the old fashioned beer gardens, custom light fixtures take their inspiration from bottle caps and they add yet another layer of warm color and pattern to the brew pub.

BACK BAY BREWING CO.

B O S T O N ,   M A

Design:
Bergmeyer Associates, Boston, MA

Photography:
Lucy Chen, Somerville, MA

The 275-seat landmark project features a state-of-the-art brewing facility that anchors the tall and dramatically proportioned main level barroom. The Brewery/Pub was designed by Bergmeyer Associates of Boston. The two levels of the pub are linked by a multi-angled wood staircase set within a generous open well that is topped by an existing gabled skylight. The street-level bar is long and additional seating is provided at movable tables. The space is almost all wood and earth tones and the tall windows, at the rear of the space, give the pub drinkers a view of the copper and stainless steel brewing vats of the brewery.

On the second level there is another bar and the seating here combines the simple wood chairs and tables with soft, plushy, upholstered chairs and sofas that look like they were moved from assorted local homes to furnish the

space. Though the wood tones predominate, there is a lively and eclectic palette used for the upholstery fabrics that along with the traditional elements suggests " a previously colorful and enigmatic history brought compellingly into the present."

Richly lacquered finish carpentry gives way to rough pine siding that has been stenciled with beer label graphics. The areas of exposed brick and the accents such as the bead board wainscotting "offer a touch of Boston familiarity."

PYRAMID BREWERY & ALEHOUSE

BERKELEY, CA

Design:
Mesher Shing & Associates, Seattle, WA

Architect:
Kava Massih Architects

Photographer:
Russell Abraham

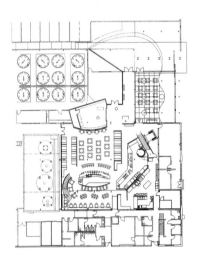

Searching for a place to put up a brewery which would be capable of producing from 8000 to 20,000 barrels annually, brought George Hancock, President & CEO of Seattle's Pyramid Breweries to the industrial area of Berkeley, CA. Hancock said, "We were looking for a transitional area with good highway access and freedom to place billboards. We also needed a location where we could afford to manufacture our product." Though there was opposition from some citizen groups who feared the area might be "gentrified," the resulting brewery/alehouse by the architect Kava Massih and the design firm of Mesher Shing not only stilled the citizens' fears but it has become a popular eating/drinking/entertainment destination in this well known college town.

Most of the four attached buildings with a total of 120,000 sq. ft. is devoted to the production of the beers that Pyramid is famous for. A corner area of 11,000 sq. ft. is reserved for the alehouse which can accommodate 250 pub-

goers on two levels. Once inside, patrons can view the continuous beer brewing process through windows that are from waist high up to 25 ft. off the ground. The giant steel tanks of the brewery, on the other side of the glass, are set below grade and lighting is kept bright for the 24-hour operation.

Robert Mesher, of the design firm, said, "We needed to make the alehouse approachable and soften the hard edge a bit. But, we also wanted to keep it real and never lose sight of the factory." The designers brought the wood roof

of the building down into the pub to warm up that space. It also added a desired, high-tech look to the alehouse. To enhance the setting, wood frames were added to the grid that separates the alehouse from the brewery. Exposed beams and pipes as well as concrete floors keep the "industrial" look intact even though the mezzanine set between the ground floor and the 25 ft. ceiling does tend to bring down the scale as it also provides more seating space. The exhibition kitchen also has entertainment value

and it underscores "the food factory" feeling.

To enhance the warmth and comfort one associates with alehouses as gathering places, the lighting is especially important. Again, according to Robert Mesher, "The track lighting and pendants give a warm glow but they still feel industrial." This "site specific" design has been very successful in attracting not only the locals but tourists with families as well. They can enjoy touring the brewery and then dining in the alehouse and still get in some souvenir shopping in the conveniently located retail shop on the premises.

TYPHOON BREWERY & RESTAURANT

NEW YORK, NY

Design:
CORE, Washington, DC

Photographer:
Michael Moran, New York, NY

Typhoon Brewery & Restaurant occupies two floors of a turn-of-the-century town house as well as part of a contiguous 45-story, highrise building on E. 54th St. in Manhattan. As designed by CORE of Washington, DC, the stonework and columns which form the exterior entrance were retained while the undistinguished infill was replaced by a contemporary glass and steel facade. It "expresses the interior organization while prominently displaying the brewing tanks to the street." Suspended over the entry vestibule is the glass and steel canopy. The muted galvanized materials used introduces the active and contemporary restaurant experience which is anchored to the tradition of brewing.

In the gut renovation of the townhouse, a large part of the second floor was removed to provide a dramatic two story high space which is edged on one side by a glass wall behind which are located the beer tanks. All action is

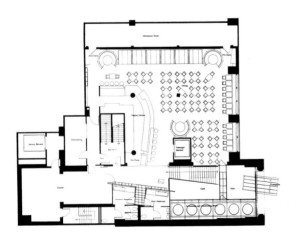

focused on the visual excitement of the brewing process and the high tech equipment. A long, serpentine shaped, zinc topped bar stretches from the entry to the rear of the space on ground level. The drinkers are faced with a warm and weathered brick wall and the structural columns and beams of the original space—as well as the brewing going on. On the right, the perimeter wall also reveals the original brickwork and there is an industrial style staircase with black metal railings that leads up to the restaurant on the mezzanine level.

A display kitchen, on the second level, provides the theater for the main dining room while the space is visually reconnected to the "raison d'etre"—the brewery—through a large opening cut into the original brick wall. Simple, light colored natural wood chairs with soft blue backs are pulled up to galvanized metal topped tables. Seating is also provided in booths along a mirror paneled wall that reflects back the open kitchen and the brewing process.

JOE'S BEBOP CAFE & JAZZ EMPORIUM

CHICAGO, IL

Design:
Aria Group Architects, Oak Park, IL

Principal in charge:
Jim Lenconi

Design team:
Grace Kuklinski Rappe / Tom Smiciklas

Photographer:
Doug Snower Photography

Growing ever more popular as an entertainment/dining/ shopping destination for locals and tourists is the renovated and expanded Navy Pier in Chicago, IL. The 7000 sq. ft. Joe's Bebop Cafe & Jazz Emporium is a combination BBQ restaurant and music venue for live jazz, swing, blues and bebop music. Located, as it is, in the heart of Navy Pier, it caters to tourists, families, young daters and music lovers of all ages and preferences.

The design concept was created by Aria Group Architects of Oak Park, IL. It has been designed to look as though the place has been around for decades and that famous musicians, whose likenesses now line the walls, probably played there many, many years ago. It is hardly a "museum" but it is a place with a "past"—a present and a

future. A 100 ft. mural on a serpentine curved wall above the banquette seating contributes to the "spirit" and the era of jazz clubs. The bright, geometric marmoleum floors help to "recall the days of old vinyl tile bars and restaurants where musicians 'sung' for their supper—because they loved their music."

JAZZ STANDARD

NEW YORK, NY

Design:
Bogdanow Partners, New York, NY

Design Team:
Larry Bogdanow / Warren Ashworth / Randi Halpern / Floriane Gremion

Photographer:
Addison Thompson, New York, NY

The two level jazz club/restaurant was designed by Bogdanow Partners of New York for James Polsky. The space on E. 27th St. afforded the architects enough space down-stairs to accommodate 200 persons listening to music—and all with good sight lines on the players. The existing elements of the upper level such as the regularly spaced

columns, high ceiling and the large skylight in the rear all gave the space "a strong, slightly industrial character—just enough to suggest an elaborated, linear interior scheme."

On the second level in the restaurant which can seat 80 in the main dining room and another 30 in the private rooms, the rhythm of the columns is accentuated by a series of elegant custom hanging lights suspended at regular intervals from the 16 ft. ceiling. While the bar and lounge are set out on a painted concrete floor, the floor in the dining room is wood. Some of the original brickwork and the concrete on the columns are exposed, but in contrast are the beautiful woods and the textiles used to upholster the chairs and banquettes. They provide a sense of warmth and comfort. The color palette is understated: soft reds and burgundies, deep sages and soft greens, mustard, gold, and dark purple—"all become fields of color against the quiet vertical and horizontal lines of the restaurant."

The designers chose to maintain the "mildly raw, gritty edge" of the downstairs area with its low ceiling and exposed pipes and ducts. These elements are softened by

the fabrics, colors and some more refined finishes. "The cultural roots of jazz and its traditional venues make an exposed ceiling especially appropriate; slightly covert, authentic, and structural. The building's systems relate to both the structure and mood of jazz music." The colors, here, are warm reds and blues plus charcoal tones. Throughout the restaurant and club paintings by Richard Polsky are visual accents and highlights. "The abstract, colorful, large-scale canvases complement the design with their quick movements, all over character and the scatty style of the interior."

MUSTARD GRILLE

TORONTO, CANADA

Design:
Hirschberg Design Group, Toronto ON

Photographer:
Richard Johnson, Interior Images Toronto, ON

Entertainment is key to the design of the Mustard Grille in Toronto. Live jazz bands fill this 30-ish, upbeat bistro setting on weekends but all week long diners are treated to the never-ending spectacle of high quality foods being prepared in the open-for-viewing kitchen. The owners asked for a design that was "fresh and artistic yet comfortable and enjoyable." The restaurant also needed to be intimate for parties of two but still able to accommodate large groups comfortably.

The sense of exuberance is evident in the jazz-oriented palette of vibrant hot and cool colors. The "cool jazz" colors of mustard, green, purple and a hot red are blended to create an exciting, upbeat spot. That color palette is juxtaposed against natural oak wood finishes which are used to "neutralize" the strong colors. The custom designed faux finishes "explode with color and vibrancy." To accentuate the 1930s jazz atmosphere, the hand painted wall murals are executed in a light wash and pictures musicians of that period playing their instruments.

The restaurant space is large and the designers, Hirschberg Design Group of Toronto, provided a variety of seating options: booths, banquettes, loose tables and chairs and bar stools. To break up the space, purple arches

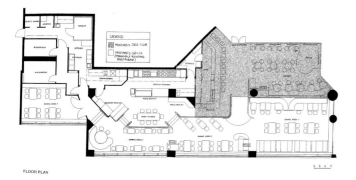

FLOOR PLAN

create the illusion of three separate dining areas in one long stretch of space. One area becomes a private dining room/wine tasting area and it features a communal table. The modular oak wine cabinets were custom designed for this area.

The restaurant has proven so successful that it has already been further enlarged with an individual jazz bar dedicated to an expanded lineup of jazz artists. According to the designers, " Plush, colorful velvet upholstery, textured faux wall finishes, flowing silk drapery—sensuality—lively colors—new forms in space—all add up to the sights and sounds of hot, yet cool, jazz." Its glamorous, lively color scheme leaves guests feeling relaxed yet energized—a state of complete well being."

GALAXY CAFE

BOSTON, MA

Design:
Prellwitz / Chilinski Associates, Inc.,
Cambridge, MA

Design Principal:
Wendy Prellwitz

Project Architect:
Bill Whitlock

Staff Architect:
Jessica Russell

Interior Design:
Susan Greco

Graphic Design:
Golinko Design, Newton, MA

Artist:
Quantum Design, Somerville, MA

Photographer:
Steve Rosenthal, Auburndale, MA

The new 13,000 sq. ft. food service facility in the Boston Museum of Science sparkles and excites as science and technology add a new dimension to the casual dining experience. In keeping with the Museum's mission, food is regarded as an educational adventure and the design firm of Prellwitz / Chilinski & Associates of Cambridge was called upon to create the visual ambiance and the stimulating setting for the four different food concepts. The food preparation process is exhibited in a series of display

kitchens and bakeries. The ingredients are on display as is the bakery producing freshly baked breads, the salads being tossed on a playful "salad bowl" counter, and pizza being flipped with flair behind a glass partition.

The focal element in all of this excitement is the brightly colored sculpture of suspended glass panels surrounding a glittering fiber optic galaxy that radiates from the ceiling. From anywhere in the dining room this sculpture draws the eye and entertains the viewer with its ever changing light play. Lighting, in general, plays a large part in shaping the ambiance from the pools of accent light on the food displays to the floating bands of blue neon. The cafe's end

walls are covered with giant photomurals of the Earth as seen from a NASA space shuttle. An arched blue wall frames the view of Boston's skyline and the Charles River.

Scattered smaller tables fill in the front part of the restaurant space "with the feeling of an outdoor cafe" and the more formal dining space offers both large and small tables in a totally relaxed setting. This area also serves as the "function" room for the Museum.

"The end result is a dining experience that offers stimulation for all the senses, a variety of options, and a menu that will appeal to both kids and adults alike."

MIRO BAR & GRILL

LONDON, ENGLAND

Design:
Corsie Naysmith, London, England

The bar/restaurant formerly located on this Fulham Rd. spot was doing very poorly. The space was taken over by the Pembertons Group and they commissioned the design firm of Corsie Naysmith, of London, to "make a miracle." The designers were expected to turn a "loser" into a "winner" with a very limited budget and in almost no time at all.

The designers found themselves faced with "a dark, gothic space with the feel of a student common room." The transformation began with walls, ceiling and ceiling rafts being painted white and extra feature lights being added. To this stark setting they added a dynamic color palette: vivid blue and a brilliant reddish terra cotta in the bar and reception areas. Opposite the bar with "a bespoke timber top round the edges," the walls were completely covered with mirror. This not only opened up the space but increased the opportunity for seeing and being seen which can be part of the fun of dining out.

With a budget of a little over $3000 to spend on props and decorative, the lead designer scoured auction houses and reuse furniture stores for bargains. He came up with old church pews, assorted mirrors and even some chimney pots which were used as planters up front at the entrance. Two new walls of banquette seating were installed and they were simply constructed. The decorative mosaic columns in the bar were finished on site with reclaimed, old sample tiles. "The reception area was allowed the luxury of new sofa, chairs, and lamp with commissioned artwork." The white walls of the restaurant provide a great background for the color filled canvases provided by local artists with the hope of selling them to the interested diners.

At last report Miro Bar & Grill is packed every night and has become a popular dining/entertainment spot on trendy Fulham Rd. in London.

INDEX BY DESIGN FIRM